ALL BLACKS
Myths and Legends

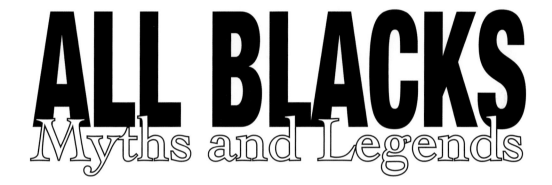

ALL BLACKS
Myths and Legends

Ron Palenski

Hodder Moa

National Library of New Zealand Cataloguing-in-Publication Data
Palenski, Ron.
All Blacks : myths & legends / by Ron Palenski.
Includes index.
ISBN 978-1-86971-144-3
1. All Blacks (Rugby team) 2. Rugby Union football players—
New Zealand. 3. Rugby Union football—New Zealand—Social aspects. I. Title.
796.333650993—dc 22

A Hodder Moa Book
Published in 2008 by Hachette Livre NZ Ltd
4 Whetu Place, Mairangi Bay
Auckland, New Zealand

Designed and produced by Hachette Livre NZ Ltd
Printed by Tien Wah Press Ltd., Singapore

Cover images: Getty and Ron Palenski

To all those who have recorded the game: if we don't know where we've been, we can't know where we're going

Contents

Preface

Like most keen followers of rugby, I'd often thought of how the All Blacks acquired their name. As a younger man, I read that Billy Wallace believed it came about as a result of a printer's error after the reporter for the *Daily Mail* referred to the team as 'all backs' because of the manner of their play. I went out to the British Newspaper Library in North London one day and had the exasperated attendant bring me a range of newspaper volumes before I was satisfied that Wallace must have been mistaken. I didn't read every word published about the 1905 tour in Britain — there was an awful lot; I'm convinced no succeeding All Black tour had such extensive coverage — but I did read the *Daily Mail* and I could find nothing that would support Wallace's belief.

Years passed and as an older man I delved into it further, helped this time by bound volumes of newspaper clippings of the tour that had been left to the New Zealand Rugby Union in Wellington. Terry McLean, with whose extensive rugby reporting career mine overlapped, was not keen on me searching for what truth may lie in the past. Hard-headed journalist he may have been at times, but there was also something of the romantic in him, as there surely is in all of us, and he quite liked the Wallace version of events and would have preferred that it remain unsullied and unquestioned.

Nevertheless, I was able to find an account of the 1905 team's first match in Devon in the local paper and, lo and behold, there were the magic words, 'All Blacks'. From the way it was written, though, it was clear the phrase was not the creation of that reporter.

Adrian Hill, a Hawke's Bay man who enthusiastically pursues the past in rugby, first alerted me several years ago to the practice in the late 19th century of teams being known by the colours of their jerseys — Wellington were the Blacks, Otago and New South Wales the Blues, Auckland the Blue and Whites, for example. From there, it was reasonable to assume the All Blacks name evolved in that way but still a first reference was difficult to pin down.

The digital age has opened wider windows on the past. A rugby and league historian in Sydney, Sean Fagan, maintains an excellent website (www.colonialrugby.com.au) on the early history of both games, especially in Sydney, and has written extensively. He excitedly emailed me one day with the news that he'd found the phrase 'All Blacks' from 1893. The reference was in a weekly Auckland newspaper, the *Observer*, the search made easier and more convenient by the excellence of the New Zealand National Library's newspaper website (http://paperspast.natlib.govt.nz). (Any rugby researcher should be familiar with the *Observer* because it was that paper and its stablemate, the *New Zealand Free Lance*, that employed George Dixon, the manager of the 1905–06 team.) Re-enthused in the search, I was able to find other references, proving beyond any further doubt that the name did indeed evolve in New Zealand and owed nothing other than publicity to British newspapers.

This was kid-at-Christmas stuff and when I told Warren Adler, the editorial director at Hachette Livre, he shared my excitement (yes, it's sad that middle-aged men get excited about such things) and came up with the idea of a book that would incorporate not just the All Black name story, but all manner of other stories about the All Blacks that have either been little told or never told at all.

This is that book. It's definitive of nothing (other than perhaps the All Blacks' name) and promises only to light a candle or two in some dark corners of rugby history.

I'm grateful to the National Library, the Alexander Turnbull Library and the University of Otago's Hocken Library for their facilities which bring the past to life, just as I am grateful to those innumerable writers, some of them named, some of them anonymous, who felt that preserving in print something of what they knew and saw and heard for future generations was worthwhile.

A South African historian, Gideon Nieman, provided the story of the selection of the 1919 New Zealand army team, the first case of racism in selection in action, for the excellent periodic publication of the Association of Rugby Historians and Statisticians, *Points Unlimited*. Other publications, especially David Kirk's autobiography, *Black and Blue*, were also useful source material. I'm grateful to those former players and coaches who helped out, especially Fred Allen, Bob Scott and John Hart, and to a former prime minister, Sir Geoffrey Palmer, who happily confirmed for me that, yes, he indeed had written a letter to the editor of *The Times* in 1967 in support of the All Blacks in general and of Colin Meads in particular.

As always, I'm grateful to Kevin Chapman and Warren Adler at Hachette Livre for their undiminished enthusiasm for rugby. Bob Luxford at the New Zealand Rugby Museum in Palmerston North again extended his ready courtesy and assistance, especially in the quest for photos rarely seen. Rugby would be much the poorer without Bob and the museum. Finally, thanks to my family, especially Kathy, who concedes the papers, books, notes and documents I have accumulated over the years can sometimes be of use.

Ron Palenski
Dunedin, March 2008

Introduction

Billy Wallace, recently returned as one of the headliners of the All Blacks' breakthrough tour of Britain and other distant parts in 1906, was safe at home when the deadly earthquake struck. Wallace was in Wellington, the earthquake in San Francisco, an ocean away.

But Wallace knew it could have all been so different. If the caprices of life had dictated otherwise, Wallace and his great mate, the All Black halfback Freddy Roberts, could have been in San Francisco on April 18, 1906 when the earth heaved and bucked, ruining a city and thousands of lives.

Fate lent a hand to Wallace, who remains one of the revered figures of the game and was the longest-lived of the Originals, as the All Blacks of 1905–06 were styled.

Their tour ended in San Francisco with two matches against British Columbia. The Canadians went south to California because their own grounds were unplayable at that time of the year and also because it was a chance to show to the University of California at Berkeley that the 'English' version of football was a safer proposition for students than the American one.

Wallace was something of a free agent during the team's swing through North America, a trip paid for by a grateful New Zealand government or at least a grateful premier, 'King Dick' Seddon. Wallace and the Taranaki wing, Jimmy Hunter, left the team at Niagara where a stop was made after an exhibition match in New York. Wallace headed to Toronto to meet relatives and Hunter went further north into Canada to see a brother.

The pair of All Blacks met up again a few days later and caught a train to San Francisco, where they arrived after the All Blacks' first match against British Columbia. Wallace was alarmed to learn that Roberts had taken ill the night of the game and a doctor was called. Roberts had trouble breathing and swallowing and a virulent form of tonsillitis was diagnosed.

The doctor was John Copeland Stinson, who had his surgery in the California Hotel, one of the grand establishments of the growing city (its population then was about 400,000). He was adamant that Roberts was too ill to travel with the rest of the team and Wallace volunteered to stay with him. Roberts was in bed when Wallace forlornly farewelled his travelling companions of the previous five months as their ship headed out into San Francisco Bay on its way to the Pacific and home.

The two All Blacks left behind were minor celebrities and Wallace enjoyed the enforced stay of three weeks, even if Roberts could not. Various local notables called to see the New Zealanders and among them were compatriots, including writer Leo Fanning, whose brother Bernard was an All Black in 1903–04, and another brother, Alf, who would become an All Black in 1913.

Another New Zealander who took the All Blacks in hand was Lucy Sargood, the wife of prominent businessman and philanthropist Percy Sargood. She learned of their presence in the city from Stinson, who was treating the Sargoods' son, Cedric, for a nasal complaint. 'Mrs Sargood was very kind to us — almost like a mother,' Wallace recalled. 'She brought us frequent gifts of fruit and flowers which were greatly appreciated. The young chap looked upon us almost as heroes and he used to stroll round with us.' Cedric Sargood was killed at Gallipoli nine years later, one of 29 Otago Infantry Battalion soldiers who died on August 9, 1915 during the disastrous assault on Chunuk Bair.

Among the locals who called in on the All Blacks was Bill Naughton, the boxing writer for the *San Francisco Examiner* and something of a celebrity in his own right. He gained the two players permanent entry to the exclusive Olympic Club and took them along to a boxers' training camp and then to a championship bout. Wallace was able to enjoy all this sightseeing and being looked after. Not so Roberts. He had to stay in bed for 10 days and when he was well enough to get out, Stinson decided Roberts would have to be separated from his tonsils.

Wallace wrote:

> He took them out there and then without an anaesthetic, and I had to sit there and see the business through. It sent a few icy shivers up my legs and up my spine. Fred was naturally not feeling too well after this and we went back to the hotel in a motor car. He had a very bad night for the throat would not stop bleeding. He became a little delirious so I called the doctor who gave him some dope, and we also got a nurse to apply some icepacks. Altogether he had a bad week.

With Roberts recovered, thoughts had to be turned to home. The next ship leaving for Auckland was the *Ventura*, a sister ship of the *Sonoma*, which had

NZ Rugby Museum

Travelling companions and great mates: Billy Wallace and Fred Roberts.

taken the rest of the All Blacks home. If they missed that, they would have to wait several weeks for the next. They were lucky they made it to the *Ventura* on time, with Wallace noting he was pleased to see that Lucy and Cedric Sargood were also passengers.

'It was a lucky thing for us that we left by this boat,' Wallace wrote. 'Had we been compelled to wait for the following boat we would have been right in the middle of the big San Francisco earthquake.'

The domed California Hotel, a city landmark where the All Blacks stayed, was totally destroyed, one of 28,000 buildings in the greater San Francisco area destroyed by the earthquake. Scientists later calculated the quake would have registered at about eight on the Richter scale of seismic energy, which was not developed until the 1930s. (Eight would have put it two points higher than that registered in 1945 for the Nagasaki atomic bomb.)

The doctor who treated Roberts, Copeland Stinson, was one of 498 people killed in the San Francisco city area alone. He was in his room in the California Hotel, crushed by falling masonry.

The dome of the California Hotel crashed down onto an adjacent fire station, killing, among others, the fire chief, Dennis Sullivan. One of the firefighters, W. A. Cook, carried Sullivan's injured wife into a safe area of the California Hotel and handed her over to a doctor.

Cook wrote in a report:

At that time, I was requested by someone in the hotel to try to save Dr Stinson, who was buried in his room on the eighth floor. I with P. Gallagher and John Coyne went at once to the eighth floor where we found that his room was full of bricks and the floor badly caved in from the heavy weight. Thinking that he might be alive, we dug for him and found him but he was dead.

Wallace and Roberts, safely back in Wellington by this time, read with horror of the earthquake and what had happened to some of those who had befriended them, and counted themselves lucky they were able to catch the *Ventura* and did not have to wait for the next ship.

So it was that two of the more celebrated All Blacks 'escaped' the great San Francisco earthquake of 1906. It was one of those stories, among many, buried in a notional archive of All Black history. For all the books written about the All Blacks over the years, from the first in 1906 until the most recent, there is still much that is untold.

All narrative histories exclude more than they can ever include. Partly that is because the writer or the historian selects what to put in and what to leave out, the process of choice conditioned perhaps by a particular point that is being made, by a word picture that is being painted of a particular tour or particular match or particular person. The further back in time the writer goes, the less available is the evidence. Sometimes there is no evidence; tales that may have been true become apocryphal, stories that could have been verified are gradually lost to succeeding generations as those who could supply the evidence die.

If teleporting humans was not a fanciful notion, historians would surely be among the first to journey back to wherever they wanted to go to establish what really happened, who really said or did what, or to seek answers to the untold number of unanswerable questions. There would be so much to investigate it would be a long time before the teleporters got around to All Black rugby.

All Blacks or those close to All Blacks are not noted for leaving much to posterity. When it was more common for people to keep diaries, All Blacks were not prominent among the daily scribblers. Reminiscences and memoirs are thin on the ground, despite what some people may think of as a proliferation of player hagiographies. Those players who have recorded the past have done so selectively for it is a well accepted adage that what goes on tour stays on tour; what happens on the field stays on the field. That is not just a rugby practice; it happens in most spheres of human activity that are recorded for later generations. Politicians have historically been much more selective about what they leave for later readers than any rugby player.

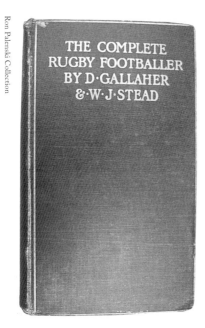

Ron Palenski Collection

The Originals' tome: the book written by Dave Gallaher and Billy Stead.

Those players who have kept their eyes open to what has been around them and written about what they have seen or done are appreciated all the more because of their rarity. Billy Stead, the vice-captain of the Original All Blacks, was among the most prolific and assiduous of chroniclers and the beauty of his writings was that they were not just about the rugby; in fact, not much at all about the rugby. His newspaper columns for the *Southland Times* throughout the tour are prized not for what they reveal about the All Blacks, but for the windows he opens on life in Britain in the early 20th century. The memoirs written by one of his team-mates, Billy Wallace, are equally valuable although, unlike Stead, they do concentrate on the rugby, as do those of a later All Black, Bert Cooke, who sheds light on the tour of the Invincibles of 1924–25.

These and the later biographies and other narrative histories unlock much of rugby's past, but there is much that is still locked away and probably will remain so. There are snatches of information passed on orally, whether from a distant or a relatively recent past, but in some cases evidence is totally lacking or in others there is a silence that has not been breached and the more time goes by, the less likely a breach will occur.

Among the great untold stories is that of Keith Murdoch. The essence of the story is well known and sometimes well documented: how he hit a security guard in the team's hotel in December of 1972 the night the All Blacks beat Wales, how he was reprimanded and named in the team for the next match, but then how that decision was overturned and he was sent home.

But he never got home, left forever to roam the Australian outback like a landlocked Ancient Mariner, although, unlike the flawed hero of Coleridge's poem, he does not tell his story. Murdoch in September of 2008 will be 65 but for New Zealanders he remains a silent 29 year old.

There are stories from tours which have not been written out of respect for the people they involved and the longer those stories go unwritten, the less likely they ever will be. They're not written down anywhere and memories are fallible things. There's a story about one All Black manager who spent a night in jail; another who, in a staggering breach of rugby protocol, charged into the dressing room just before a test and started making demands about travel arrangements for the following day.

There's also an unprovable but nevertheless delightful story about an All Black selector choosing a player for a team and on meeting him at training, asking who he was. When told, he realised he had picked the wrong man.

Then there are purely match stories which enter rugby folklore and can never be proven one way or the other. The most notable of those is the Bob Deans non-try of the 1905 test against Wales, but just about every All Black could tell a tale of a try that should, or should not, have been scored; or a kick that did, or did not, really go over.

Into that latter category comes a Bledisloe Cup test in 1991 at Eden Park, the last before the World Cup. The Australians won the first test in Sydney 21–12. A fortnight later, the All Blacks won 6–3, two Grant Fox penalty goals to one from Michael Lynagh. That's what the referee decided and that's what the records show. But late in the match Lynagh had another kick at goal and the ball just dropped over the crossbar. To the quiet amusement of a couple of the All Blacks standing in their in-goal area, the kick was deemed to have missed. They knew different. Lynagh's kick, they saw, had gone over and the All Blacks gained a win that should have been a draw.

Newspapers reflect the present and can unlock the past. They are a prime source for what happened long ago and the distinction between fact — or at least what a newspaper reporter was told was fact — and opinion is usually clear. It is sometimes an aid to credibility to know who the reporter was. A prolific columnist in the *Otago Witness*, for example, went by the name of 'Forward' and he wrote copiously on all manner of rugby topics, never afraid to air his opinion or to criticise rugby authorities if he felt they got something wrong. He was in a position to know because 'Forward' was James Hutchison who held various positions in the Otago Rugby Football Union and was editor of the *Otago Daily Times* for 37 years. He would never have had any trouble acquiring inside knowledge.

Newspapers also create. It has been commonly held that the All Blacks had their nickname bestowed upon them by British newspapers because of the colour of their playing uniform. This occurred during the 1905–06 tour. It is true that the phrase 'All Blacks' gained its first frequent and wide usage during that tour but it was not the invention of any British reporter.

As has been noted before, it was common for teams in the late 19th century to be known by their jersey colours; New South Wales and Otago, for example, were often referred to as the Blues. Wellington played in black and they were known as the Blacks. For a time, they also had black shorts and it did not take a great leap in creativity for the name All Blacks to surface. For all the talk of inspired originality by British reporters or for talk of printers' errors turning 'all backs' into 'All Blacks' the evidence about the origin of the rugby world's most famous nickname lies firmly within the tightly packed columns of 19th-century New Zealand newspapers.

How the All Blacks got their name is one of the rarely told, or never told, stories which follow.

Black in the 19th Century

It seems an odd thing that for a name as uniquely and distinctively New Zealand as the All Blacks, its origins remain clouded. In attempting to explain its origins, shattered myths are still recycled. But the name is an evolutionary tale and it is now possible to roll back a few more years.

It has until now been accepted that the name was coined, or at least gained a wide currency, during the pioneering tour of Britain, France and the United States in 1905–06. The latter part at least is true — it was only during and after the tour by Dave Gallaher's team that the players were habitually referred to as All Blacks.

But the name was not coined then. It is at least as old as the national team itself and appeared in print long before 1905.

It was Billy Wallace, the longest-lived of the Original All Blacks, as the 1905 team came to be known, who was responsible for the most common and enduring myth about the origins of the name. And because it was one who was there who did the telling, it was believed and even now, when his story has been discredited, it is still repeated and perpetuated.

His story, first made public in July of 1964, was that the name was the result of a printer's error. After New Zealand beat Hartlepool in the 11th game of the tour, the *Daily Mail* reporter who covered most of their matches, J. A. Buttery, wrote that the whole team, backs and forwards alike, played with such speed and precision it was as if they were 'all backs'. Somehow an 'l' was inserted and the name became 'All Blacks'. Or so the myth would have us believe.

The Original All Blacks pose for the camera early in the tour while in Devon.

The story gained official endorsement when it was repeated in the government-sponsored *New Zealand Encyclopedia* in 1966. The players, according to the encyclopedia, arrived in Taunton to play Somerset and saw posters welcoming the 'All Blacks'. Buttery made inquiries and, so the story goes, reported to the team that the poster printer had inserted the 'l'. This was repeated, but the lack of evidence was noted in the *Oxford Dictionary of New Zealand English*.

But there is a problem with that oft-told tale. Buttery's coverage of the Hartlepool match makes no reference to 'all backs'. The *Northern Daily Mail*'s Football Edition, a paper like the old sports papers in New Zealand that was rushed into print as soon as possible after Saturday afternoon matches, covered the match comprehensively. Down in the 15th paragraph, the paper precedes a list of the players' weights with the comment: 'A glance at the undermentioned weights of the invincible "all blacks" will convey some idea of the calibre of the team.'

Those indefatigable compilers of New Zealand rugby history, Rod Chester and Neville McMillan, also fell into the Hartlepool trap, writing in *Centenary* that the term 'All Blacks' in the *Daily Mail* report was 'probably' its debut in print.

Wallace remarked on the Somerset posters when he wrote his memoirs for the *New Zealand Sportsman* in 1932:

> As we drove through the town to the hotel we saw the town placarded with posters advising the people to 'come and see the wonderful All Blacks play'. The name 'All Blacks' had now stuck to us. It is the name with which we were christened by the *Daily Mail* and it caught on with the general public, though quite a number were misled into thinking we were a team of black fellows.

There was no mention of 'all backs' then, no mention of a rogue 'l', but a belief that the *Daily Mail* was responsible for the name.

It was not, however. Further research of newspaper files showed that the name was used for the first time in a report of their first match, long before Hartlepool or Somerset. After Devon had been beaten 55–4, a local paper, *The Express and Echo*, reported next morning: 'The All Blacks, as they are styled by reason of their sable and unrelieved costume, were under the guidance of their captain (Mr Gallaher) and their fine physiques favourably impressed the spectators.'

The name did not recur in print until the Hartlepool reference but thereafter it became more common and first appeared in a heading in the *Daily Mail* on October 19, 1905, a week after Hartlepool and a month after Devon.

The Devon paper's wording, 'as they are styled', implies that the name had been used even before then.

Journalist and author Terry McLean, whose rugby coverage spanned 60 years, attempted to explain how this was so. In the last book he wrote, *The All Blacks*, published in Britain in 1991 to coincide with the World Cup in

Britain, he told how two newspapermen were on the tender that greeted the All Blacks' ship when it arrived off Plymouth at the start of the tour. McLean's version of events is that one of the reporters asked a player about the team's uniform: its jersey, its shorts, its socks. To each question, the player answered with one word: black.

'The conversation ended,' McLean reported, 'when the player, in a burst of eloquence, remarked, "We are all black".'

McLean, with liberal journalistic licence, then wrote of how the reporter heads for his office and is secretive 'until the triumphant moment when he lays before his sports editor the item which leads off by proclaiming that "the All Blacks have arrived"'.

It might have been like that but there is no evidence. It is curious that McLean, an author of about 30 books and writer for the *New Zealand Herald* whose first rugby touring experience was in 1930, had not reported this incident before.

Before leaving Britain, it's worth recalling there was some truth to the 'all backs' story but a complete reversal of how it was perpetuated. About the time the Originals were in Scotland for their first test, vice-captain Billy Stead reflected on the tour so far in his weekly column in the *Southland Times*. He wrote about the All Blacks' unbeaten record to that point and told how British writers were trying to work out why the team was so good.

'The nearest guess to the secret of our success,' he wrote, 'was by a well known army officer who suggested the altering of the name All Blacks to "all backs" for, he said, the moment the ball is secured or lost in the scrum then the whole fifteen "sweeps" seem to be backs.'

There was another reference to 'all backs', this one in the *Daily Chronicle* report of the match against Oxford University which looked towards the match against Cambridge University:

I see that Cambridge are to employ the device of five threequarters and seven forwards in tomorrow's match and this seems to be a move in the right direction for the scrummage is the merest detail in New Zealand football. At the same time, even five threequarters, plus the two halves, cannot be regarded as possessed of the capacity to cope with a team who, ignoring all the traditional theories, convert themselves into all backs.

There is ample evidence that the All Blacks name was in use before the team arrived in Britain. A backward progression, if such an oxymoron is permitted, shows that the New Zealand team was referred to as the All Blacks in 1904. On June 28, the Sydney correspondent of the *Evening Post* in Wellington previewed the imminent arrival in New Zealand of the British team that had played in New South Wales. Assessing New Zealand's prospects, he wrote: 'If the New Zealand forward team is as good as it ought to be, I think the chances favour the "all blacks".' The lack of capitals would have been a decision made at the *Post* since telegraphic transmission did not distinguish between upper and lower case letters.

The phrase also appeared in the Auckland weekly newspaper, the *Observer*, earlier that month but in a report of a club match between City and Suburbs. 'The red and blacks did not have it all their own way, the all blacks playing up with great determination,' it commented.

It was a common practice in the late 19th and early 20th centuries for newspaper reports to refer to teams by their colours. Since that is so, it is reasonable to assume that newspaper reporters did not act in isolation and that identification by colours was also a part of everyday conversation. In a modern highly communicative world, it is instructive to recall that 100 and more years ago, apart from telegraph, the only methods of transferring information from one person to another was by speech or by writing: no radio, no television, no other means of disseminating information.

It is now common knowledge, after first being reported as late as 1992, that the Original All Blacks' manager, George Dixon, referred to his team as 'the Blacks' in the copious diary notes he kept throughout the tour. The phrase did not begin with him.

The real Originals: the 1893 team, the first chosen by the New Zealand Rugby Football Union.

It was first used in relation to the first official New Zealand team, that is, the first chosen under the auspices of the New Zealand Rugby Football Union. That team toured Australia in 1893 and played a shake-down match against Wellington before departure.

The Wellington Rugby Football Union *Annual* of 1894 in a reference to that match said: 'The Blacks (ie, the New Zealand representatives) won . . .' The parentheses were the *Annual* editor's. Later in the same report, the writer said: 'The Blacks now played up with great determination . . .'

In July of 1893, when the team was in Australia, the *Auckland Weekly News* commented on the first match against New South Wales, which the New Zealanders lost: 'The Welshmen played better than their supporters expected, but the blacks were the better team.' (Again, no capitals).

A fortnight after that, the *Observer* in Auckland previewed the second of the matches against New South Wales:

Next Saturday, the deciding match against New South Wales takes place, and with this last success fresh on their memories, they should require nothing more to urge them on and despite the gruelling they got at last meeting, I expect to see the all blacks [no capitals, no quotation marks] come out on top with a substantial majority.

Curiously, the *Observer* had run a full-page cartoon a fortnight before depicting the 'stale' players before, during and after their loss to New South Wales. They were not all black at all. Cartoonist William Blomfield showed them accurately in black jerseys with a silver fern and white knickerbockers — precisely the uniform their captain, Tom Ellison, had persuaded the New Zealand union to adopt at its first annual meeting earlier that year.

The real genesis of the phrase 'All Blacks' lies not with the national team at all, but with Wellington and the so-called New Zealand Native team that toured Britain and Australia in 1888–89, each of them drawing on the habit of referring to a team by its colours.

Wellington then played in black jerseys, black shorts and black socks and while they were most often referred to as the Blacks, they were also on occasion 'the All Blacks', such as in this passage from the *Evening Post* previewing a match against Auckland in August of 1889: 'Many people are of opinion the boys will have their hardest struggle with Wellington, and although an old Wellingtonian myself, I think the "all blacks" should be pleased if they can obtain a draw against the "blue and whites".'

Wellington were not always black, though. The Natives played Wellington before leaving on their tour and the Natives had the prior claim on black because their jersey was what would

Again New Zealand reps. have met Queensland, and again they have administered a decided defeat. The score of 35 points to nil is certainly a monstrous one, and when we think of the hollow victory of Canterbury reps. against Auckland last season and consider that they only scored 23 points, one can easily imagine the runaway victory the New Zealand boys had last week. Next Saturday, the deciding match against New South Wales takes place, and with this last success fresh on their memories, they should require nothing more to urge them on, and despite the gruelling they got at last meeting, I expect to see the all blacks come out on top with a substantial majority.

An Auckland weekly newspaper, the *New Zealand Observer*, mentions 'All Blacks' for the first time.

Ron Palenski Collection

later become New Zealand's — black with silver fern. Wellington obligingly changed to blue and white stripes similar to Auckland's colours and match reports of that game, and of others, referred to the Natives as 'the Blacks'.

It becomes abundantly clear from irrefutable evidence that the name All Blacks preceded the 1905 team, though it gained a wider acceptance during that tour, largely through the agency of the multiplicity of British newspapers.

Tom Ellison, who died before the name gained wide usage, was a pivotal figure. He played for Wellington when they were 'all black', he was one of the leading figures in the Natives team and it was he who transferred the Natives' jersey to the shoulders of all who played for New Zealand, and then captained the first New Zealand team to be known, if only briefly, as All Blacks.

One of the few New Zealand academic sports historians, Greg Ryan, wrote a master's thesis at Canterbury University in 1992 about the Natives. He called the thesis *The Originals*, but when the thesis became a book a year later, the title changed to *Forerunners of the All Blacks*. He was close to being right the first time. In terms of the rugby world's best known nickname, the 1905–06 players were not the Originals at all.

For King (Dick) and Country

Richard John Seddon was the longest serving prime minister — though he was known as premier — of New Zealand. He headed his Liberal Party government from 1893 until 1906 and, for a time, introduced a range of groundbreaking social legislation, including votes for women. Seddon was an imposing man physically: just under six feet tall and a weight that ranged from 15 to 20 stone. A larger than life figure, his girth constantly stretched the fabric of the frock-coats he habitually wore.

Lancashire-born and raised on the West Coast of the South Island, Seddon's personality was as domineering as his size. There was seldom any doubt that the party and government bent to his will and, towards the end of his tenure, parliamentary opposition was ineffectual. Seddon was the most dominant political leader New Zealand has had: more than Savage, more than Holyoake, more than Muldoon or Lange, more than Clark.

Seddon was that peculiar product of the late Victorian-Edwardian era in colonial New Zealand: a nationalist imperialist. He was fiercely proud of his adopted land — he took the credit for coining the phrase, 'God's own' — but he was just as fiercely loyal to the Motherland and to its far-flung empire.

His political antennae were acutely tuned and when he sensed an opportunity in the wind for promoting New Zealand, especially in or for Britain, he took it. It was almost Seddon alone who committed New Zealand troops to the Boer War; the most distant colony rallying to the Empire's cause.

And it was almost Seddon alone who committed the taxpayer to underwriting the cost of the Original All Blacks' return from Britain through North America. Correctly divining the popularity and patriotic pride in the team that beat everyone but Wales, Seddon dispatched the All Blacks homeward across the Atlantic partly as thanks from a grateful government but also as a promotion for New Zealand.

Long before the word 'marketing' entered the rugby lexicon, long before commercial organisations lined up to ride on the All Blacks' coat-tails, Seddon saw the publicity value of success in sport.

Amid a flurry of books published in New Zealand in 2005 to mark the centenary of the Originals' tour, one of them remarked, 'The genesis of the American venture is rather obscure.' But it wasn't.

As early as May 1905, two months before the All Blacks left Wellington, the New Zealand union turned down a request from the British Columbia Rugby Union for the team to play in Vancouver on the way to Britain. Undaunted, the Canadians repeated their plea, urging New Zealand to 'help us along in our fight to popularise the finest of winter games'. They dangled a substantial carrot:

> Of course we would give you very liberal terms; almost anything to get a game and as the Dominion Fair is being held in New Westminster — a town 10 miles away — this summer, the chances are that you would reap considerable pecuniary benefit by a game either in Vancouver or New Westminster, in September on your way over.

Little more was heard until December, shortly before the Welsh match, when the New Zealand union cabled the Originals' manager, George Dixon, and suggested he should investigate the possibility of returning via the United States and playing exhibition matches there. This was at a time of growing concern, led by President Theodore Roosevelt, about the brutality of the American brand of football and the New Zealand union clearly thought this might give rugby a foot in the door. Dixon was empowered to see if he could borrow a few British players to join the All Blacks in American exhibitions, but the English union was not keen and a week later Dixon cabled Wellington that the idea was impractical. 'A similar impression prevailed amongst the management committee of the New Zealand Rugby Union prior to receipt of the cablegram,' the *Evening Post* remarked.

A fortnight later, with the All Blacks by then in France on what they thought was the last leg of their tour, Seddon came up with his plan. Newspapers reported this dispatch from Greymouth:

> Ministers have under consideration a proposal (if it can be arranged) for the New Zealand football team to come back to the colony via Canada and America, the expense to be borne by the colony. It would be a treat for them and a courtesy and mark of appreciation by New Zealand of the worthy manner they have represented New Zealand football in the Mother Country.

Parliament was not sitting at the time and the phrase, 'ministers have under consideration', can be taken as code for Seddon having it under consideration. Why else would such a dispatch come from Greymouth?

Far from being a treat for the All Blacks, as Seddon thought, the idea was not greeted warmly at all.

The most assiduous chronicler among the players was Billy Stead, the Originals' vice-captain and strategist. 'We had all congratulated ourselves on coming through an arduous tour, and we think it rather hard of our union to call us into the field,' he wrote in one of his regular columns for the *Southland Times*.

The manager, Dixon, was even less impressed with the largesse of the government. Within three days of Seddon's message from Greymouth, the New Zealand union at an informal meeting in Wellington accepted the offer and cabled Dixon, telling him to organise matches in Canada and the US.

Premier Richard John Seddon on the hustings in Wairarapa in the late 1890s.

It formalised the decision three weeks later, as the NZRFU's minutes record:

The action of an informal meeting held 2nd Jany 06 called to consider correspondence between the Hon the Premier and Mr Campbell in accepting the Govt's offer to bring the team back via America and passing resolution to be conveyed by Mr Campbell to the Premier, 'That this Committee desires to express its high appreciation of the Government's generous offer' was confirmed.

(George Campbell acted as chairman of the union while Dixon was away.)

Once back in London after the Paris trip, Dixon wrote to the New Zealand union secretary, Edgar Wylie. 'I must confess to a feeling of disappointment,' he said, 'when I received instructions for the American route. At that time I was fully convinced that it would be impossible because of weather and conditions to play matches in either Canada or America and I was looking forward to the six weeks quiet and rest of the steamer.'

Dixon listed a few injuries among the players and added:

> The rest of the team are all well though heartily tired of football. Personally I am very glad the tour is over. It has been a long and heavy task. There is no doubt that the programme was a bit too heavy and as we all along foresaw, it was a mistake to have the Welsh matches at the end of the tour.

Dixon again aired his frustration at the direction he and his team were bound to follow when he wrote in his private (and unpublished) diary on January 5: 'This trip is a confounded nuisance.'

The government's direction, for that is what in effect it was, was not greeted with universal acclaim in New Zealand newspapers either. It is necessary to understand, though, as some of the 2005 celebrants did not, that newspapers then were much more overtly politically aligned than they are now and, indeed, some newspapers such as the *Dominion* two years later were founded by politicians. Newspapers were either for or against Seddon and the Liberal Party; it followed therefore that the anti-Seddon newspapers were also critical of the government bringing the team home via North America. Such opinions were reserved almost exclusively for editorials and rarely exposed in reporting of events. As one reporter, Guy Scholefield, later recorded: 'In most offices, both upstairs and down, were staff members opposed to the policy of their paper. New Zealand has acquired a reputation offering haven to journalists whose opinions were disapproved of by their employers.'

To catalogue newspaper criticisms of the North American venture and interpret them as widespread opposition is to somewhat miss the point. The criticisms, when the knowledge of how individual newspapers viewed Seddon is taken into account, were predictable.

The *Evening Post*, for example, was long an opponent of Seddon's and, indeed, had been the only daily paper to mount a campaign five years earlier in favour of New Zealand joining the Australian federation (to which Seddon was opposed). The *Post* called the trip a 'national picnic' and 'a wicked waste of public money'. While it paid due regard to the successes of the footballers, it said:

> The truth is the Premier is playing to the football gallery, which may applaud the proposition; but though it is naturally just now a very enthusiastic gallery, it does not represent the taxpayers of the country, who should not be compelled to provide the means for a piece of foolish extravagance.

Similarly, the *Otago Daily Times* opposed the trip, saying it was the New Zealand union rather than the team that was benefiting from the government's generosity. The other daily paper in Dunedin, the *Evening Star*, supported Seddon, as did the *New Zealand Times* in Wellington. All newspapers fell into well-worn lines.

One newspaper which may have been a little confused about what line to take was the weekly *Observer* in Auckland, which was not above puncturing Seddon's ego when it felt a need to do so. But the *Observer* was owned by the company of which the All Blacks' manager, Dixon, was a senior executive, so it came down on the footballers' side.

Whether holiday or work in the United States, the paper believed the All Blacks deserved the gratitude of their government. 'Triumphant footballers are the best of all immigration agents,' it said.

Dixon's views had clearly got through to his employers, though, because the paper published a full-page cartoon depicting Seddon handing a bandaged and sore-looking Dave Gallaher a ticket for a trip through Canada and the United States. It ran a caption saying:

> King Dick (to the New Zealand rugby captain): Congratulations, my fine

fellow. You and your team have done splendidly. Now, I propose, by way of holiday, to send the team through Canada and America to play some more matches.

Captain Davy Gallagher [*sic*]: Holiday, you call it. Surely, bruised and battered as we are, we have played enough football for the honour of New Zealand. Anyhow, we want to get home.

Ron Palenski Collection

How the *Observer's* cartoonist, William Blomfield ('Blo') saw Seddon's sponsorship of the All Blacks' visit to North America.

Dixon was able to arrange three matches in the United States, but none in Canada because of frozen grounds. Instead, the Canadians went to California and two matches were played against British Columbia in San Francisco as 'missionary' games to show Americans how much more attractive (and safe) rugby could be than the American version of football. The other game was an exhibition in New York at a baseball field in Brooklyn against a team grandly styled as 'All-New York' but which in fact comprised seven of the New Zealanders (including coach Jimmy Duncan) and eight expatriate Britons. Dixon was the referee. The *New York Times*, noting that about 500 spectators saw the game, spent much of its report outlining the differences between 'the English game' and American football. 'The absence of any kind of defensive armour is a distinctive feature of the New Zealanders' appearance,' it said.

Stead thought the crowd was twice the size the *New York Times* estimated. Though tired, he clearly saw the game as something of a novelty and a chance to introduce rugby to Americans.

The team, though wearied with a satiety of football, readily fell in with the proposition and with the help of eight British rugby players resident in New York, to whom we loaned seven players (all we had available), a match was played on Thursday, February 1. We marked out the ground ourselves, and the twelve hundred who viewed the match were mostly comprised of sporting editors and, what was more important, college experts. The passing and kicking delighted them and as we played the game as open as possible we felt that we had done good work in this, our first missionary effort.

Developing Commercialism

In the days immediately preceding the World Cup in France in 2007, newspaper companies confronted the cup organisers over their plans to restrict the use of photographs from the event, especially on websites. Similar disputes have occurred at other international sports events.

The issue is money and marketing. Both sides want to make as much money as they can from an event — organisers by retaining and controlling rights to what they grandly call their 'intellectual property' and newspapers by selling more newspapers or by increasing use of their associated websites.

It seemed on the surface to be a particularly 21st century sort of dispute, involving as it did the rapid development in the latest of technology as well as the all-pervasive hand of marketers and lawyers in modern sport.

But the essence of the argument has been around a long time. The Originals' tour of Britain in 1905–06 was threatened by what today would be called a media blackout.

In 1905, the New Zealand Rugby Union tried to control who took photographs of the All Blacks and when and where those photos were published. This was at a time when press photography was still very much in its infancy and the only New Zealand newspapers to regularly publish photographs were weeklies, especially the offshoots of the major dailies: the *Weekly News* in Auckland, the *Weekend Press* in Christchurch and the *Otago Witness* in Dunedin. The photos were generally grouped together in separate sections printed on special paper. There were others, among them the *New*

Key figures in rugby's early dash for cash – George Dixon (left) and Neil Galbraith.

Zealand Graphic and the *New Zealand Illustrated Sporting and Dramatic Review* in Auckland, *New Zealand Free Lance*, *New Zealand Mail* and *New Zealand Referee* in Wellington.

In the daily newspapers, photographs were a rarity for another decade, although they were more common in 1905 in Sydney and in Britain, as the New Zealand Rugby Union knew.

The All Blacks' most celebrated tour, that of Britain in 1905–06, was preceded by a three-match money-making venture to Sydney with a game in Auckland before and matches in Dunedin, Christchurch and Wellington after. The whole purpose was to make enough money to cushion any financial ill effects of the British tour (which turned out to be much more lucrative than anyone thought).

As part of the push for profit, the NZRU's management committee — a Wellington-based committee that took care of the union's day to day business — decided a week before the visit to Australia to call for tenders for the sole right of taking photographs of the team. The committee knew what it was doing because it was chaired by George Dixon, who managed the team in Britain but who, more significantly in this context, was well versed in the newspaper industry, which was much more competitive then than it is today when there is only one daily in each town. Yorkshire-born Dixon, who came to New Zealand when he was 19, qualified as an accountant and managed the weekly *New Zealand Observer* in Auckland before moving to Wellington to help establish the *New Zealand Free Lance*.

A member of the committee that decided to call for tenders was the union's treasurer, Neil Galbraith, who was also manager of the All Blacks on the quick trip to Sydney.

The players went for a training run the day they arrived in Sydney and photographers were told they were not welcome unless their employer paid for sole rights. One of them was from the *Sydney Mail*, the assistant editor of which was Ernest Hoben, who confronted Galbraith. Hoben spoke with the authority and experience of a newspaper executive but also from the high ground of being the man who more than any other single individual had caused the New Zealand union to be formed 12 years before.

Galbraith told Hoben he would have to write to Wellington to complain, which Hoben did. In his letter to the union secretary, Edgar Wylie, he said, 'I cannot conceive that the effect of this has been fully considered by your union. I am writing at once lest the team goes to England unfairly handicapped.'

The thrust of Hoben's argument was that the team needed newspapers more than the newspapers needed the team — later to be a familiar argument, if seldom heeded, in rugby. Whatever the union was able to gain through selling photographic rights, he argued, it would still be dependent on the income from gates and it was only publicity generated through newspapers that would make people go to watch.

By refusing photographers permission to take pictures of the first training, the team forfeited, according to Hoben's estimate, about £30 or £40 worth of advertising.

Hoben wrote:

Newspapers will not submit to what you propose. And as one who was responsible for the creation of the New Zealand union I am sorry that such a thing was ever done. New Zealand newspapers, also Australian, have given many hundreds of pounds' worth of valuable space to the New Zealand union and its games and football generally free, space which others would have had to compensate for by equivalent advertising.

He said he and other New Zealanders in Sydney, including another journalist, Charlie Marter, who started Billy Wallace off on his football career, felt the union's bid to flog off rights to picture the team was as bad from a business point of view as it was from an amateur sport standpoint.

Hoben was as concerned about the implications in Britain as he was for the effect in Sydney where, it had to be said, he had a vested interest in open access to the team.

'You must remember that the papers can still get along without illustrating the team,' he wrote. 'The team cannot make a financial success without illustrations. Papers . . . will simply kill the team by ignoring it and if it is not illustrated in leading papers, people will think it is because it is not a first-class affair.'

Hoben knew what he was talking about, as events proved. The team, once the rights idea was dropped, was lavishly illustrated in Britain and without question the publicity helped make the Originals' tour the success — financial and playing — that it was. Leading London-based papers, especially the *Daily Mail*, the *News Chronicle* and the *Daily Mirror*, gave the All Blacks immense photographic coverage, sometimes filling the whole of their front pages with pictures of the team. It is entirely reasonable to conclude that no subsequent All Black team in Britain has received such coverage in newspapers.

Hoben in Sydney had support from the New South Wales union, which

NZ Rugby Museum

If the New Zealand union had had its way, newspapers would have had to pay for this photo of the New Zealand and New South Wales teams in 1905.

was keenly interested in the gate and therefore in as much pre-match publicity as the team could gain.

As Galbraith dolefully noted in a letter to Wylie:

> The New South Wales officials fear that if the local papers do not get the team for their papers that a considerable amount of gate money will be lost by this means of advertising, and further that we will suffer in a literal way as well as receiving a very much curtailed notice in the papers.

He said he had talked to Jim Henderson, who had managed the New South Wales team in New Zealand in 1901, and said he felt that the £100 being asked for the rights would not 'account for the deficiency caused in not advertising the team by means of a photograph and in conjunction with the support of the local papers'. Galbraith urged Wylie to seek a reconsideration of the union's decision at its next meeting.

After the tour, Hoben again wrote to Wylie, thanking him for his explanation: 'I was merely desirous that nothing should be done to prejudice the success of a team going from a union which I had the honour to found and in whose welfare I always take the keenest interest.'

Scots' Amateur Stand

As unlikely as it may seem, a bunch of Scottish cricketers once tried to do what the New Zealand and England rugby unions could not do and what the Scottish union would not do — get the All Blacks of 1924–25 to play in Scotland.

The 1924–25 team, the second from New Zealand to tour Britain, came to be known as the Invincibles because, unlike their predecessors, they beat everyone they met. But they did not meet Scotland or even set foot in Scotland. That cost them the chance of a grand slam, for which New Zealand rugby had to wait another 54 years.

The reason they did not go north of the border was because the deeply conservative Scottish union bore a grudge against England. There was also residual resentment by the Scots about the 1905 All Blacks, but it was perfidious Albion the Scots really had a snitcher on.

The tours by the Original All Blacks in 1905 and by the Australians in 1908 led to suspicions by the Scots that the 'colonial tours', as they were known, were taking rugby down the ruinous road of professionalism.

Both the New Zealanders and Australians happily acknowledged players were paid a daily allowance of three shillings — hence the All Blacks' proud description of themselves as 'three bob a day men' — and this was done with the full knowledge and blessing of their hosts, the English union.

It was also done in the full knowledge that when British teams were in New Zealand or Australia, the same thing applied. The difference was that while the New Zealanders and Australians called their payments a daily allowance, the British teams called them 'wine money'.

The Scottish union saw the daily allowance as a breach of the amateur ethic that it so jealously guarded. The leading figure in the English union, George Rowland Hill, was described by *The Times* in its obituary of him as 'amateur of amateurs and Tory of Tories'. His equivalent in Scotland, an accountant called George Aikman Smith, took the defence of amateurism to an evangelical level.

When Smith died five years after the Invincibles' tour that he blocked, the *Scotsman* noted of him: 'Always a strong upholder of the pure amateurism in Rugby Union football, Mr Smith took part in many a keen fight when he and his committee felt that this principle was either being violated or was in danger of infringement.' Among other things, he was opposed to numbers on the backs of playing jerseys. 'It's not a cattle market,' he once famously remarked.

Smith liked to be known as Aikman Smith, just as Hill liked his surname to be recorded as Rowland Hill. The Australian captain in 1908, Paddy Moran, with that Australian talent for pricking pomposity, simply called the Scot 'Jock Smith'.

After the Originals' tour Smith nagged and nagged the English union for a full copy of their financial accounts so he could scour them for evidence that the players were paid to play. Eventually, three years after the tour, the accounts were delivered and Smith felt vindicated. The first entry on the debit side of the accounts read plainly: 'To daily allowance to players, £1042 9s 0d.'

The Scottish union acted. This was early in 1909 and its ruling committee, of which Smith was then secretary, promptly announced it would not play England in the annual championship match scheduled for March. The Scottish view was that since the New Zealanders and Australians were 'professionals' with the connivance of the English union, it automatically made the English union professional as well.

The *Scotsman*, the august Edinburgh daily not given to overstatement, headlined the Scottish union's response boldly: 'A Rugby Football Sensation. Rupture Between England and Scotland. International Match Off.'

NZ Rugby Museum

The 1924–25 team that became the Invincibles, though they couldn't prove it against Scotland.

It then recorded Smith's statement:

The immediate cause of this serious decision is that my Committee [its capitals] have only now learned, in response to their request . . . for the accounts of the New Zealand team which visited this country in 1905, that each member of the team, in addition to being allowed every possible expense, received an 'allowance' of £1 1s per week for himself. At the same time, they have learned that the players of the Australian team presently in this country received a like 'allowance'. These 'allowances' being cash payments which the players can either spend or save, my Committee are unhesitatingly and unanimously of opinion that they are contrary to the principle of amateur Rugby Football and, in short, amount to professionalism. The English Union have written to the Scottish Union . . . stating that these 'allowances' have been made with the approval of the English Committee.

Such was the import of the story, in Scotland anyway, the *Scotsman* wrote an editorial about it. It thought the New Zealand transgression on its own may just have caused disagreement between the two British unions but the question 'has been placed in a much more serious light by the admission of the English Union that the payments to which exception has been taken were made with their approval, and that the Australian team which is now touring in England and Wales are receiving the same licence'. It said the Scottish union had no alternative but to break off playing relations with England.

All of this incensed the New Zealand union's man in London, Charles Wray Palliser (another who liked to use three names). He was a public servant who worked in the New Zealand High Commission (and was later briefly High Commissioner) and sat on the English union committee as a New Zealand representative. (The International Rugby Board, though in existence for more than 20 years, was still trying to work out what its role was. Its sole purpose at the time was to arbitrate on disputes between national unions, usually over interpretations of playing laws.)

Palliser wrote a letter to the editor of the *Scotsman* to protest against 'the unsportsmanlike action of Scotland's Union in seizing so frail an excuse to make England the scapegoat for the presumed evil doings of New Zealand'.

He said he thought there was much that Scotland was not saying and the Scottish attitude went much deeper than the professed horror at the payment of daily expenses.

That the Scottish Union has a very strongly expressed dislike for visiting teams from our colonies coming over here is most evident . . . and I have no doubt . . . that this question has long been the subject of very many discussions with the Scottish Committee, who have been waiting the opportunity for striking at England, the leader of imperialism in sport.

Palliser did not hold back in laying out what he saw as Scotland's motivation for its attitude to England.

Up to the year 1905 the Scottish Union made no objections and placed no obstacles in the way of playing members under her Union joining teams under the Rugby Union [England] and paying visits to the Colonies. In fact, Scottish players took a leading part in these tours and were everywhere well received and hospitably treated by our Colonies.

(The British team in New Zealand in 1904 was captained by a Scot, David Bedell-Sivright.)

Palliser argued that the Scottish union was put out not so much by the All Blacks being paid a daily allowance, but by the union itself not cashing in on the success of the All Blacks' tour. He then raised a series of questions:

1. Why did Scotland refuse to give New Zealand a small guarantee for the test in 1905?
2. Why instead did Scotland offer the whole gate to New Zealand before it had ascertained just how popular the All Blacks were?
3. Why did Scotland not regard the match against the All Blacks as a full international?
4. Why did the Scottish union show a lack of courtesy to the New Zealanders during their time in Edinburgh?

Palliser did not attempt to answer his own questions but the implication was clear: the Scottish union was still simmering with resentment about not making any money out of the All Black test while the New Zealand union gained £1710 2s 5d. He was much blunter in a letter to the secretary of the New Zealand union: 'It is, of course, obvious that the action of Scotland is a reprisal for the supposed wrongs she suffered at the hand of New Zealand.'

England and Scotland eventually agreed to take their dispute to the International Board, which met in early February 1909. The board then comprised only the four British unions — Ireland sided with Scotland and Wales with England. So there was an impasse.

But as Palliser wrote in another letter to Wellington:

A resolution was, however, unanimously carried to the effect that no daily allowance shall in future be paid to players coming here from the Colonies. . . . as far as I can see, it will make little or no difference except throwing a lot of work on the manager in paying all small extras incurred by the team which hitherto has been covered by the daily allowance.

Scotland argued that the ban on allowances should have been made retrospective but eventually it compromised. The Scotland–England match went ahead the following month.

Another outcome of the dispute was that the International Board decided in 1911 any future tours by 'the colonies' should not be arranged by England alone and that each of the British unions should have a say in when tours would take place, by which country, and detailed matters such as itineraries, accommodation and travel. Also agreed was that each of the unions would pay a £750 guarantee for any future tour.

And this was what led directly to the absence of the All Blacks from Scotland in 1924.

In the early 1920s, Scotland spurred on by Smith worked towards building Murrayfield, having outgrown its earlier ground at Inverleith, where the 1905 All Blacks played. It was heavily in debt to pay for Murrayfield (which opened in March 1925) and clearly did not see the prospect of the All Blacks in 1924 as bringing enough money through the gate to reduce the debt. Neither, apparently, did it see the benefits of bringing the Murrayfield construction forward so that Scotland could play the All Blacks there as an opening game.

Late in 1923, the Scottish union sent a statement to all its clubs:

In July 1923 your committee were more than surprised to be advised that the RFU were bringing over a New Zealand team in 1924 and were asked if they wanted fixtures. This arrangement was so absolutely opposed to the agreement formally come to . . . and would naturally open the way to any of the four countries having the right to entertain a touring team for their own profit, that they [the SRU] promptly declined to entertain the proposal and, in any case, no fixtures would have been arranged by your union, even if willing, under the financial arrangements which they understood were laid down by the RFU.

The Scottish union's annual meeting in 1924 was held, unusually, in private but it made a public statement afterwards in which it was said the union had no quarrel with New Zealand. As the *Scotsman* reported:

It was shown that it was the English Union that Scotland had a grievance against in that they had taken upon themselves the making of all arrangements for the New Zealanders' visit, which was against an agreement come to some years ago, when it was decided by all the countries — England, Scotland, Ireland and Wales — that in future all tours, either from Britain or to Britain, should be under the auspices and control of the Rugby International Board [its words]. Obviously there had been a breach in that agreement and because of that the Scottish Union Committee had decided to decline the two matches with the New Zealanders offered to them by the English Union.

The closest the Invincibles got to Scotland was to Carlisle, often described (from the English side) as the last town before Scotland. There they beat Cumberland and in a report of the match in the *Scotsman*, the unidentified writer said a visit to Scotland was still a possibility.

'A movement is on foot to bring the New Zealanders to Edinburgh and the Scottish Rugby Union have, it is understood, been asked if they would have any objection to such a match being carried through.'

The report said the Lord Provost (mayor) of Edinburgh, Sir William Sleigh, was keen on the idea.

As close to Scotland as the Invincibles got. Captain Cliff Porter in the action against Cumberland at Carlisle.

This is where the cricketers come in. The newspaper report did not say, but it may have been referring to a plan by the Carlton Cricket Club of Edinburgh to get the All Blacks to their city.

Carlton, named for the arch-conservative 'gentleman's' club in London, was an inner-city cricket club in Edinburgh catering to the city's well-to-do. It won the first unofficial Scottish club championship in the early 1920s and an indication of its preferences was that it was noted Carlton 'won its distinction without professional assistance'. The club in 1924–25 was trying to raise funds to buy the ground it rented, and this may have been a factor in its rugby interest.

Around the time of the All Blacks' visit to Carlisle in late October 1924, the club applied to the Scottish union for permission to stage a match in Edinburgh between the All Blacks and a Scottish XV.

The union, not surprisingly, turned the application down. As the *Scotsman* noted, 'That would seem to put an end to a widespread hope that the All Blacks would, after all, be seen in Scotland.'

Ironically, Scotland had their best team for years that season and probably had a better chance against the All Blacks than any of the other national teams. The Scots went unbeaten through the 1925 international championship, as it was informally known, winning the title for the first time since 1907 and gaining their first grand slam. They scored a total of 77 points, nearly twice as many as the next best, and 17 tries, while England, Ireland and Wales were next with nine each. The Scots fielded a threequarter line that is still regarded fondly in Scotland. All four players were from Oxford University — Johnny Wallace, Ian Smith, George Macpherson and George Aitken. For all the Scots administration's disdain of colonials, Aitken was a New Zealander who captained the All Blacks against South Africa in 1921, Wallace was an Australian and Smith was born in Melbourne.

The Scots still have never beaten New Zealand.

Even the admirable Aitken had to be defended against British accusations of professionalism when he arrived in England in 1922 to take up a Rhodes scholarship. Newspapers suggested that he, like other New Zealanders, took money when it was on offer and this incensed Palliser's successor as the New Zealand union man in London, Wanganui-born solicitor Cecil Wray.

He wrote a letter to the editor of *The Times* saying Aitken's reception in England caused great resentment in New Zealand. He was put through a special form of inquisition merely because he was a colonial (though New Zealand had ceased to be a colony 14 years before).

Wray wrote Aitken felt deeply humiliated by his critics and asked: 'Do they not think a young man who has earned a scholarship under the conditions laid down by that great Empire-builder Cecil Rhodes is entitled to better treatment when he comes as a keen student and an enthusiastic amateur sportsman to the place we in the Dominions call Home?'

'87 — How the Cup Was Won

When the Australian referee Kerry Fitzgerald blew his whistle for the last time in the World Cup final in Auckland in 1987, John Reason of the London *Daily Telegraph* turned to his neighbour in the Eden Park press box and said: 'Well, that was the bore of the century.'

Reason had watched a lot of rugby over the years so his experience and knowledge could be respected. His judgment, at least when it came to New Zealand rugby, was another matter.

An hour or so later, the victorious All Black captain, David Kirk, a dribble of blood still visible as testament to the battle glorious, was asked by another English journalist, Tony Bodley of the *Daily Express*: 'David, do you think that match was worthy of a World Cup final?'

Kirk slowly shook his head and half-smiled. 'You guys make me laugh, you really do.' (It is a nice irony that 21 years later Kirk heads the Fairfax media organisation which employs hundreds of 'you guys'.)

The match of the tournament, perhaps still the match of any World Cup, was the semi-final the week before when France somehow snuck a win over Australia at Concord Oval out in the west of Sydney by doing what only the French seem able to do. Kirk and other All Blacks, then and later, readily acknowledged the magnificence of that semi-final.

But the point of the exercise was to win the final, and this the All Blacks did against a French team that could not shoulder the burden of their glory

David Kirk kisses the Webb Ellis Cup (again) for photographers. On the right is Graham Mourie, one who advocated the introduction of a World Cup.

across the Tasman. Not even France could play like that two Saturdays in a row (although they went close seven years later when they beat the All Blacks in successive weeks). Cup horrors against France were well into a black hole of an unimaginable future.

The All Blacks have lost their way and some of their aura in every World Cup that has followed but in 1987 they set the standard for a new rugby world that embraced the concept of a global tournament for the first time.

Winning was not enough for those All Blacks; they needed to show to themselves, to New Zealanders and to the rest of the world that they were taking rugby to a higher plane, that by pursuing their unattainable goal of playing the perfect game a win would be a by-product, not the goal.

It was as if they knew, as some of the more perceptive probably did, that the World Cup would eventually usher in a brave new world of professionalism and that force of numbers in other rugby countries would eventually count against New Zealand. Even the rugby gods are on the side of the big battalions.

The first World Cup was the first chance for New Zealand, and perhaps the last, to point the way to the future, to lay down a template for a changed rugby world.

In the week before the pool match against Fiji in Christchurch, the All Black coach, Brian Lochore, and his two offsiders, John Hart and Alex Wyllie, had a drink before dinner in the hotel then owned by the former international referee Tom Doocey. The bar was crowded and rugby talk was in the air; it was a top-drawer hotel, but a rugby pub nevertheless. One of the drinkers — and this was early in the evening so wisdom was not yet obtained from a glass — was of the opinion that the cup would be won by either Australia or France. The All Blacks, he said, had been impressive in their pool matches but just wait until the 'real' matches started.

The three All Black coaches heard all of this and stayed mute, smiling with an inner knowledge that they knew something not many other people did. This All Black team was something special and if the general public had not realised that yet, they soon would.

A confluence of factors marked out the first cup for the All Blacks in a way that could not be replicated for any other country, no matter how well prepared they might have been. And some of them were not prepared well at all. Ireland arrived not wanting a cup at all. Writer and former player Derek Wyatt in his history of the cup related a story about the Irish centre, Brendan Mullin, who was worried about Ireland's chances in the first pool match against Wales. 'We must beat them if we are to progress,' Wyatt quoted Mullin as saying. This ignorance of tournament play seemed to typify the British and Irish attitudes to the cup. It was just another tour; the only difference was everyone else was on tour as well.

New Zealand knew different. The selectors, probably still the best selection panel New Zealand rugby has had, figured out what was needed long before the cup started. It was late in 1986 that Lochore, Wyllie and Hart settled on their selection philosophy: pick a team of 15 players and then add others as back-ups and utilities. It was not a touring squad that was needed; it was a tournament squad. Teams were being asked for the first time to win six successive test matches if they were to win the cup. It was a foreign concept to the rugby mind as it was conditioned then. Other countries have since fully grasped tournament needs but the fact remains New Zealand was there first (even if some of the lessons have since been forgotten).

It was not just understanding what a cup required that gave New Zealand an edge. There was also the recent history of the continuing sore of playing against apartheid South Africa. The cancelled tour by the All Blacks of 1985 and the subsequent rebel tour in 1986 by the Cavaliers split not just the country asunder but rugby as well.

The government led by David Lange was deprecating of rugby every chance it got and rugby, since 1981, had just a tenuous hold on its status as the national sport that helped shape the New Zealand identity. When the rebels were reintroduced to the mainstream in mid-1986 for the last two tests against Australia and later in the year for the tour of France, player animosity ran deep.

David Kirk, who had been captain for the domestic tests and was then supplanted for the French tour by Jock Hobbs, wrote of the fraying of his youthful idealism and how he was reduced to tears after the loss in the second test in Nantes, such was the ferocity of the barbs hurled his way by some of the rebels. (Kirk's mood would hardly have been helped by his choice of tour reading matter. Most players, then and now — and probably earlier too — immersed themselves in airport novels. Kirk read Fyodor Dostoevsky's dark and depressing *Crime and Punishment*, which portrays the murder of a miserly pawnbroker and her younger sister by a destitute student and the emotional, mental and physical effects that follow.)

In the summer of 1986–87, therefore, New Zealand rugby had the twin clouds of the loss in Nantes and a divided camp. It was not the type of background upon which a successful assault on rugby's first World Cup could be easily overlaid. Lochore thought the French tour had stilled ill feeling between the rebels and the others but the loss in Nantes, as Kirk demonstrated, brought the issue to the surface again. Bitterness can spring from the depths of despair.

By the end of 1986, New Zealand had its new selection panel. Lochore was still convenor and his two new assistants were Hart and Wyllie, hugely successful coaches of Auckland and Canterbury. When they met before Christmas, they talked at length of the need to play a 'new' game, one based on possession and pace, underlaid by extreme physical fitness, and to choose players best suited to the type of game they envisaged rather than to simply choose the best players. The distinction was understood by the three men who had the destiny of New Zealand rugby in their hands.

Nantes was in the background as a rallying call, a battle cry: 'Remember Nantes!' It was there too as a reminder of what the French could do when they were in a mood to do it. It was not lost on the three selectors that the first match in the cup would be the first since Nantes.

The rebels were in the background too. As the 1987 season unfolded, and as the matches between the North, South and Central zones were played, and the South Pacific championship that involved only Auckland, Canterbury and Wellington unfolded, those close to the centre of things wondered how the Cavaliers would be dealt with. The intensity of feelings of just a few months before could not simply be forgotten as if they never existed.

The captaincy of the cup squad exercised minds. The most recent All Black captain was one of the rebels, Jock Hobbs, who had held out the hand of friendship and support to Kirk in France. The rebel captain, and a former All Black captain, was Andy Dalton. He had not been in France and it was evident that he was close to retirement and, but for the lure of the cup, may well have retired.

By the time of the final trial in Whangarei, Hobbs had spared the selectors a conundrum by announcing his retirement. They chose Dalton because of his proven leadership ability.

Ron Palenski Collection

The 1987 World Cup squad. Back row: Andy Earl, John Kirwan, Albert Anderson, Gary Whetton, Murray Pierce, Alan Whetton, Zinzan Brooke, Wayne Shelford. Third row: Joe Stanley, John Drake, John Gallagher, Michael Jones, Richard Loe, Bernie McCahill, Kieran Crowley. Second row: Neil Familton (physio), David Kirk, Grant Fox, Warwick Taylor, Mark Brooke-Cowden, Bruce Deans, Craig Green, David Laing (doctor). Seated: Brian Lochore (coach), Sean Fitzpatrick, Steve McDowell, Andy Dalton, Frano Botica, Terry Wright, Richie Guy (manager).

Any residual feelings about the rebels were addressed by Hart at one of the first meetings of the cup squad. In effect, he gave the players the same message Abraham Lincoln had delivered in a speech about slavery more than a hundred years before: 'A house divided against itself cannot stand.'

Then there were the players. Crucially, Lochore, Wyllie and Hart stayed faithful to their belief in picking players capable of playing the type of game they wanted. They wanted a fullback who could defend but also one who could enter the line at pace or double round outside his wings. They wanted a first five-eighths who could exercise iron control, who would be cool under pressure and who could move the ball quickly. And so it went on: job descriptions for every position.

It meant some All Blacks of the past were discarded — the hard-as-nails flanker Mark Shaw among them — and some players of whom the country had barely heard were introduced: Michael Jones and Zinzan Brooke, among others. (Shaw was staggered by the physical intensity demanded by the occasion. After one of the zone training sessions, a drained Shaw exclaimed, 'They blow your arse!')

Players were also chosen because of their attitude and demeanour, players who could comfortably accept that though they were in the squad, they might not play. Two of them, Bruce Deans and Frano Botica, did not.

Neither did a third. Andy Dalton's hamstring tear at training on the North Shore in Auckland in the week before the first match is now a part of rugby lore. Kirk was moved up to the captaincy and stayed there as Dalton struggled to regain fitness and, when he did, it was too late for him to be included. By then, the All Blacks were on a roll.

There was a curious disagreement between the selectors in Christchurch before the Scottish quarter-final, though, when it became known that Wyllie wanted Deans to be given a chance at halfback. Hart was opposed and Lochore stayed with the status quo. Who would have then captained the All Blacks in Kirk's absence was not discussed.

Kirk was at risk for another reason, one that has barely surfaced in the retelling of the golden months of May–June 1987. Late in the last pool match against Argentina in Wellington, Kirk was hit hard by an Argentine flanker, Alejandro Schiavio. From the grandstand, Kirk looked groggy. The game ended soon after and two of the All Black forwards, John Drake and Alan Whetton, raced to Kirk's side and escorted him from the field. The doctor on standby at the ground, Bill Treadwell, went to the All Blacks' dressing room to attend to Kirk but was not allowed in. A half hour or so later, Kirk emerged for press interviews and assured everyone he was fine. It was a good act. He was not fine at all. He had been briefly unconscious and was concussed, as he years later conceded. Had that been publicly acknowledged at the time, Kirk would have had to stand down for at least the next match — the quarter-final.

The All Blacks needed Kirk, as they well knew. Not just because of his leadership on the field (Dalton still provided valuable off-field guidance) or for his speed and skill as halfback, but because he was, unwittingly and probably unwillingly, providing New Zealand rugby with a fresh face. For a nation used to its main sporting heroes being described, not always incorrectly, as unsmiling giants, the image of the All Blacks was now presented with an elfin mien.

As the chairman of the New Zealand union, Russ Thomas, remarked unblushingly: 'Older women want to mother him and younger women want him to make them mothers.'

Not just on the field but off the field as well it was all starting to come together for the All Blacks and for New Zealand rugby. The success of the World Cup as a tournament, and the success of the All Blacks in particular, helped bring people back to rugby, helped restore rugby as a source of pride rather than as one of shame, embarrassment or anger.

Before the final in Auckland, Lochore and the players were much taken by the number of people, unable to get tickets to the match at Eden Park, who lined the road outside their hotel, the Poenamo, on the North Shore and who cheered them through the streets of Auckland and as they arrived at the park.

Lochore recalled:

I needn't have bothered with a team talk. The people of New Zealand were saying it all. It was there for all to see and hear. The players knew. They were playing for the people outside the hotel, the people in the streets, the people outside the park, the people inside, the people at home watching on television. They were playing for all New Zealanders everywhere.

The revelation of the 1987 World Cup, Michael Jones, in the opening match against Italy.

The All Blacks had not been able to say that for several years.

And was the final worthy of a final, as Kirk was asked? The All Blacks were as dominant as they had been throughout the tournament, taking a grip on possession and using their loose forwards and backs to apply the pace. They scored three tries to one and the final score of 29–9 did not wholly reflect their command.

The answer lies not so much in what happened at Eden Park in 1987, but what has happened at subsequent finals. Four tries were scored in the 1987 final — more than has been scored at any final since. In the five finals since, only five tries have been scored. As has become plainly evident, finals are won by teams with the best defence. They are matches to be won regardless of any wider aim.

Gerald Davies, the fine Welsh and Lions wing who became a perceptive and articulate writer on the game, echoed his English colleagues in 1987 when he wrote that the tournament that year deserved a better final.

'The disappointment rests in that the All Blacks gave themselves no opportunity to explore any further potential they may have,' he wrote in *The Times* on the Monday after the final.

Davies could not have known it, but the All Blacks explored their potential over the next three years and fashioned one of the greatest records of any All Black team.

By then the four-year cycle of cups had begun and New Zealand had had its day in the sun.

When Club and Province Collide

Rugby is supposed to be the ultimate of team games, all for one and one for all, looking after your mates and all that sort of stuff. It may be the ideal, but it has not always been the practice.

A strange clash between club and parochial pride and a peculiar brand of rugby politics once led to a team of footballers going on strike at the same time as putting the national team in jeopardy.

It happened in Wanganui in 1923 when New South Wales were touring New Zealand and after a New Zealand Maori team had been in Sydney.

Wanganui in early August of 1923 had a squad ready to go north to play matches against Bay of Plenty, Thames Valley and Auckland but, on the point of departure, four of the players withdrew, saying they would rather play for their club, Rata in the Rangitikei sub-union.

The Wanganui union acted promptly and suspended the sub-union as well as the four players. It seemed, on the surface and in the initial newspaper reports, to be purely a local affair.

But once the names of the players were published, it became a national issue. Two of them, Peina Taituha and Pat Potaka, were also members of a New Zealand squad of 20 that had been named to prepare for the first of three unofficial internationals against New South Wales. Taituha had not long returned from Australia with the Maori team.

The New Zealand union was told of the suspensions. What transpired between officials in Wellington and Wanganui has not survived but four days

NZ Rugby Museum

NZ Rugby Museum

Peina Taituha (left) and Pat Potaka.

later the players were censured and the suspensions lifted. Instead, three officials of the Rangitikei sub-union were suspended until the end of the year.

Wanganui meanwhile went ahead with their tour and beat Bay of Plenty, but lost to Auckland and Thames Valley.

Potaka and Taituha, who was also known as Taituha Peina Kingi but whose name was more commonly published at the time as simply Peina, were free to join the rest of the New Zealand squad in Timaru, where they trained at Caroline Bay for the week before the international in Dunedin.

Potaka and Taituha (though listed as Peina) both played in the Dunedin match, won 19–9 by the All Blacks.

The squad stayed together for the second match the following week in Christchurch but in the meantime their Wanganui colleagues were still not happy. They decided to withhold their labour. 'Footballers strike' was the headline in the *New Zealand Times*, which was then a morning daily in Wellington.

The other two players who had put Rata ahead of Wanganui, and who had been briefly suspended, were still in the Wanganui squad for a match against Hawke's Bay and the rest of the Wanganui players said they would not play. They named Potaka and Taituha as well as the other two as the players they objected to, even though the two All Blacks were still with the national team preparing at New Brighton in Christchurch for the second match against New South Wales.

The harassed Wanganui officials tried to sort it all out. As the *New Zealand Times* said:

> A deputation set off on a 30-mile journey to interview two of the players who had refused to appear tomorrow, but a broken down lorry on a narrow road made it necessary for the deputation to retrace its steps for six miles and conduct an interview per medium of the telephone.

The negotiations succeeded, the players withdrew their strike threat and Wanganui went ahead and played Hawke's Bay at Cook's Gardens, losing 16–6.

The match in Christchurch two days later went ahead too with the All Blacks this time winning 34–6. Taituha was normally a second five-eighths but this time played on the wing. Potaka went on as a replacement.

Neither covered themselves in glory. 'Peina [Taituha] is not a wing threequarter, that much is evident,' the 1905 All Black, Ernest Booth, wrote.

Booth, who had worked as a journalist in Australia and Britain after retiring from rugby, was even harsher on Potaka: 'Potaka gave a poor exhibition and was not even up to representative standard.'

Neither Taituha nor Potaka were asked to play for New Zealand again, though there was no suggestion the Wanganui shenanigans had anything to do with that. They were in fact in good company.

Whatever the origins of the adage about never changing a winning team, it certainly did not originate with the 1923 selectors, Alf Griffiths of

Wellington, Wally Drake of Canterbury, Ned Parata of Horowhenua and Donald Stuart of Otago.

When they named their team for the third match against New South Wales, there was only one survivor from the All Black team that had won so well in Christchurch.

The reason for all the changes, New Zealand union chairman Stan Dean was forced to explain, was that the selectors wanted to see as many players as possible before thinking about their team for the much greater mission, the tour of Britain the following year.

There's nothing modern about the accusations of handing out All Black jerseys. Whatever they did, and regardless of the results against New South Wales, the selectors were not popular chaps.

Hawke's Bay even wrote a letter of protest to the New Zealand union about the selection of one of their players, Sam Gemmell, out of position. He was normally a loose forward but had been played at hooker in the first international in Dunedin.

'It is patent to the veriest tyro that possession of the ball in an international match is absolutely essential,' the Hawke's Bay union said in its letter. 'The action of the selectors in playing Gemmell in the front row requires an explanation as the position is absolutely foreign to him.'

It added that Gemmell's unusual placement meant that the halfback, Jimmy Mill, another Hawke's Bay player, did not get the opportunities he should have had.

'A strong feeling prevails throughout Hawke's Bay that our representatives have not received fair play, as in every representative match our forwards have overwhelmed the opposition yet in the second test we have not a single representative.'

Hawke's Bay held the Ranfurly Shield at the time.

The letter also, rather snidely, said the union 'would be glad to receive an assurance that Mr Dean was not a fifth party on the New Zealand selection committee'.

Hooker 'Bull' Irvine is bowled in the All Blacks' North–South cricket match at Days Bay where they trained before their third match against New South Wales in 1923.

Dean said he had not been present at any of the selection meetings. 'The position was that if a deadlock between the four selectors arose, a member of the New Zealand Rugby Union was to be called in; but that position has not arisen,' he said.

It wasn't just Hawke's Bay who were upset with the selectors. Waikato also complained, saying that with all the changes for the third 'test', it was hoped at least one or two players from their area might have been included.

'The New Zealand union should wake up to the fact that Waikato is in New Zealand,' the union said.

Undeterred, the selectors assembled their charges at Rona Bay, near Eastbourne across the harbour from Wellington, for a week's training before the third match. Alf Griffiths was in effect the coach of the team, though not named as such, and their fitness trainer — though that term was many years away from being coined — was a Wellington athletics expert, Dorrie Leslie.

This was in the days when British rugby authorities decreed international teams could not assemble more than 48 hours before a match and it was common in Britain for players to drift into town the afternoon before a test. Not so in New Zealand. The All Blacks' days before the Wellington match were carefully regimented by Griffiths and Leslie.

The wakeup call each day was at 7 am and the first joint activity was a walk along the beach at 7.15. Breakfast followed and after that and for the rest of the morning, there was rugby-specific activity. After lunch, there was more physical work but the players were encouraged to play cricket if the weather was suitable or billiards if it was not. There was haka practice before the evening meal and, after that, players were confined to their accommodation. Lights were put out at 9.30.

Despite all the team changes, the All Blacks won the third 'test' even more convincingly than they had the other two. New South Wales were beaten 38–11.

Results Better Than Ever

When the denizens of the International Rugby Board took the big plunge in 1995 and wiped out everything they once held dear by declaring the game 'open', they changed rugby forever.

It was the biggest change made to the game in its history. It dismantled at the stroke of a pen and with the unified nodding of greying heads the structure on which the game had been built, sometimes painfully and always deliberately, for the previous hundred or so years.

No one then could foresee the effects of the change, other than for the short term, which was that players would be paid to play the game they were good at by anyone who could afford to.

A few wise old heads — Russ Thomas, the former chairman of the New Zealand union among them — shook in dismay, lamenting that it would eventually be the ruin of the game.

Those of a more nationalistic bent, eschewing any altruism about the good of the game, worried that the rich would get richer and the poor would, if not get poorer, at least stay much the same. God would once again be on the side of the big battalions. The bigger and more populous the rugby country, the more they could afford to pay their players and the stronger they would be.

It wasn't just the direct influence of money; not just England players driving to training in a BMW or a Rolls-Royce rather than working out which train would get them there on time. It was also the indirect influence.

Players paid for playing wouldn't have to have a real job, indeed, wouldn't have time for a real job. They would therefore while away their days on the training field, in a gym or stuck in front of a computer terminal going through the process that some now know as analysis by paralysis.

That was a far cry from the amateur days when England players in particular would show up at the team's hotel perhaps the day before the match, have a bit of a yarn and a bit of a chuck around and perhaps discuss a tactic or two.

None of this was good news for New Zealand, even though New Zealand with its southern hemisphere mates in Australia and South Africa provided the catalyst for the IRB to show that it could follow if not lead.

New Zealand is small. Big perhaps in rugby terms and no international team in the world has a record better than the All Blacks, but small in just about every other sense. A couple of poxy islands was how the Wales assistant coach, Scott Johnson, once put it. Take out the adjective and he was right. New Zealand is not just small, but isolated. Miles from anywhere.

Those in New Zealand who could see beyond the goal-line could see that rugby in countries such as England and France would have to improve with professionalism; money would ensure that happened and what New Zealand could generate by comparison would be minimal.

British rugby writers such as Stephen Jones, who loves New Zealand almost as much as he loves baiting New Zealanders, would have salivated at the prospect of the All Blacks being humbled. When England had one of its rare wins over New Zealand at Twickenham, Jones looked as if he'd just won Lotto. And he's Welsh for goodness' sake. He's the John Reason of his era. (During the first World Cup, after a dispute about whether players could endorse products, Jones wrote that it was difficult to uncover just what it was All Blacks did for a living — 'the team seems largely free from career pressures, the traditional barrier in many British sports to sporting excellence'. Jones could have asked Craig Green what he did for a living while Green waited on a bus on the Monday morning after the cup final to take him to work.)

One of the key figures in the All Blacks' continued ascendancy, Dan Carter, against Italy in Rome in 2004.

So the gap would close. Money not just ended a hundred years of amateurism, it could also have ended the dominance the All Blacks have had since they first set football boot on British soil. British and French rugby especially had money, earned directly such as sponsorships and television rights and other purely rugby revenue, as well as wealthy backers queuing up to bankroll clubs which had hitherto been struggling.

New Zealand, with a population a fraction the size of Britain's and with a structure that does not allow private investors (not that there was any sign of willing takers), clearly would find it difficult to compete.

But has the gap closed? There's ample anecdotal comment that it has, that New Zealand rugby is not as strong as it once was, that the All Blacks are not as hard as they once were ('hard' in the physical sense and hard to beat), and that generally New Zealand since the advent of professionalism has slipped from its lofty perch.

People who mount such arguments point to the World Cup and say, in effect, 'If All Black rugby was still dominant in the world, why have they won the World Cup only once?'

The World Cup, as much as the All Blacks would like to win it again and as much as they have tried to do so, is not the sole measure of international rugby success. Rugby has not yet copied other elements of soccer and deemed all international matches to be 'friendlies' unless they are part of some organised tournament. Test matches outside of World Cup matches still do matter and as long as television continues to shell out for the right to show them, and as long as people still want to watch them, as long as third-country venues such as Hong Kong still want to showpiece the Bledisloe Cup, test matches will matter.

If the World Cup is the Everest of rugby endeavours, a test match is just a Hillary Step away.

There's no evidence that the All Blacks have slipped; quite the reverse in fact.

By the end of 1993, six years after the first World Cup and when the end of professionalism was nigh, the All Blacks had played 277 test matches and won 199 of them with 64 losses and 14 draws. That gave them, from their first test in 1903 until their last in 1993, a winning percentage of 71.8.

Fourteen years later, the All Blacks' winning percentage has increased to 74.1 — 318 wins from 429 matches with 94 losses and 17 draws.

The All Blacks have improved their winning record since professionalism.

Statistics are not everyone's measuring rod of choice and they were certainly not for Mark Twain who said there were three kinds of lies: 'Lies, damned lies and statistics.' But he was far from being a rugby man and it wasn't even the rugby season when he littered New Zealand with his bon mots in 1895.

The statistics which tell the numeric history of the All Blacks are plain and simple. A win is a win and a loss is a loss. The All Blacks have many more of the former than of the latter and continue to do so — no statistical chicanery about that.

A little deeper look through the records shows that the modern All Blacks — overpaid, overrated and over here, as one unkind British commentator once remarked (at least he left out the other 'over' from the original line as it applied to American troops in Britain in the Second World War) — quite comfortably stand comparison with any of their predecessors.

Break the All Blacks' record down into eras. The first is from the first test in 1903 until the start of the First World War in 1914. That shows a winning record of 79.1 per cent. The second era covers between the two world wars and the All Blacks slipped to 52.7 per cent, largely attributable to the advent of South Africa and also to the playing confusion after the dropping of the distinctive wing forward position.

The third era is from the end of the Second World War until the 100th test at the end of 1959. The winning record there is 65 per cent.

The next era, from 1960 to 1969, was the All Blacks' most dominant, most of it under coach Fred Allen. Their record for that period was 83.3 per cent.

It slipped again from 1970 to 1979 when the winning record was 62.2 per cent, but then rose again to 78.9 per cent for the 1980–89 period that included the first World Cup and the unbeaten 22-test run under Brian Lochore and then Alex Wyllie.

From 1990 until the last of the amateur years, 1995, the record was 74.5 per cent. It rose marginally for the rest of the 1990s to 75.6 per cent (and certainly wasn't helped by the five successive losses in 1998).

Since 2000, the All Blacks have played 93 tests and won 77 of them, a winning percentage of 82.7, second in these groupings only to the teams of the 1960s.

Cynics will argue but oh yes, in that time they played teams such as Portugal and Fiji and Samoa and any number of other supposed minnows. Yes they have, but in the same period they have met much more frequently their stronger opponents such as Australia, South Africa, England and France.

Peter Bush

The dominant figure of Alex Wyllie supervises a scrum session.

England, with all their greater playing resources and riches, have been able to make little impact on the All Blacks under professionalism. Of the 29 times they have met, England have won just six — and only two of them (2002 and 2003) were in the professional era. It's worth adding that Ireland and Scotland are still waiting on their first wins against New Zealand and Wales haven't beaten the All Blacks since 1953. Their combined might as the Lions have won a series in New Zealand just once and their only tour in the professional era was a failure.

For most of the 20th century, the All Blacks and the Springboks were regarded, rightly, as the heavyweights of world rugby. Their irregular series were billed by journalists as being for the mythical world championship. New Zealand for much of that time lagged behind South Africa and indeed, at the end of 1993, their winning record against their most formidable foe was a miserable 42.1 per cent.

But since professionalism, the All Blacks have raced away, despite losses to South Africa in the last few years. The All Blacks have won 24 of 34 since 1994 for a percentage success ratio of 70.5 per cent.

If a gap has closed since money has washed through the game, it has closed only across the Tasman. Between 1903 and 1993, the All Blacks and the Wallabies met 97 times for 66 New Zealand wins — a percentage of 67. Since 1994, though, the Australians have closed the gap like no other team. Of 31 tests since then, the All Blacks have won 14 and their winning ratio drops to 61.2. But it is still at a healthy and respectable 66.4 per cent overall.

New Zealand's overall test winning record of 74.1 per cent is infinitely better than any major opponent's. South Africa are next best at 63.2 per cent, France at 54.9 per cent, England at 53.1 per cent and Wales at 51.5. The rest are less than half.

Professionalism has bitten into New Zealand rugby, there's no doubt. There's a continual outpouring of players to where they can get more money and there's a constant strain on the budgets of the national and provincial unions to pay players enough to keep them in New Zealand. But for the magnet of the All Black jersey, more players would be lost.

It may be that in the future, unless the national and international structures of the game undergo radical change, New Zealand will be even more disadvantaged and the All Blacks will suffer. But, in the meantime, the All Blacks are as dominant as they have always been. They just can't win the World Cup.

ALL BLACK TESTS						
	Played	Won	Drawn	Lost	For	Against	% (of wins)
Argentina	13	12	1	–	585	180	92.3
Australia	128	85	5	38	2395	1656	66.4
Britain (Lions, Anglo-Welsh etc)	38	29	3	6	634	345	76.3
Canada	4	4	–	–	234	39	100
England	29	22	1	6	652	364	75.8
Fiji	4	4	–	–	304	36	100
France	46	34	1	11	1122	599	73.9
Ireland	20	19	1	–	517	199	95
Italy	9	9	–	–	597	96	100
Japan	1	1	–	–	145	17	100
Pacific Islands	1	1	–	–	41	26	100
Portugal	1	1	–	–	108	13	100
Romania	2	2	–	–	99	14	100
Scotland	26	24	2	–	744	285	92
South Africa	72	40	3	29	1289	1081	55.5
Tonga	3	3	–	–	238	16	100
United States	2	2	-	-	97	9	100
Wales	23	20	-	3	693	216	86.9
Samoa	4	4	-	-	207	42	100
World XV	3	2	-	1	94	69	66.6
	429	318	17	94	10795	5302	74.1

COMPARATIVE RECORD OF MAJOR OPPONENTS		
	Played	Won	% (of wins)
South Africa	356	225	63.2
France	634	348	54.9
England	601	319	53.1
Wales	582	300	51.5
Australia	479	238	49.7
Scotland	566	241	42.6
Ireland	565	232	41.1

COMPARISONS OF SUCCESS				
Period	Tests	Won	Drawn	Lost	% (of wins)
1903–1914	24	19	2	3	79.1
1921–1938	36	19	2	15	52.7
1946–1959	40	26	1	13	65
1960–1969	42	35	3	4	83.3
1970–1979	45	28	3	14	62.2
1980–1989	57	45	3	9	78.9
1990–1995	51	38	1	12	74.5
1996–1999	41	31	1	9	75.6
2000–2007	93	77	1	15	82.7
Totals	429	318	17	94	74.1

AGAINST SOUTHERN RIVALS				
	Tests	Won	Drawn	Lost	% (of wins)
Australia					
1903–1993	97	66	5	26	68
1994–2007	31	19	–	12	61.2
Totals	128	85	5	38	66.4
South Africa					
1921–1993	38	16	2	20	42.1
1994–2007	34	24	1	9	70.5
	72	40	3	29	55.5

'ANZRFU' — It Almost Happened

The selection of Robbie Deans late in 2007 as the Australian coach, as unprecedented as it was — and the added piquancy it was given by his failure to become the All Black coach just the week before — was merely another link in the chain that winds back to the formative days of rugby in both countries.

An added dimension, one that reinforced the great circle of life that is rugby, was Deans being a grand-nephew of Bob Deans, the All Black in 1905 who thought he scored against Wales and thus helped create a powerful folklore.

The connections between New Zealand and Australian rugby have been close and constant, as befitting two isolated neighbours in a far-flung rugby world. Australians have played for the All Blacks and New Zealanders for the Wallabies (and some have played for both); New Zealanders have captained Australia and the reverse is also true; a cross-Tasman rugby traffic has been one of the enduring characteristics of the relationship.

A rugby fan and former prime minister, Mike Moore, once remarked of New Zealanders' attitudes toward Australians: 'They are our best mates, whether we like them or not.'

An Australian High Court judge, Michael Kirby, who was once an advocate of New Zealand becoming an Australian state (or two states, actually), spoke in 2003 of the trans-Tasman relationship and quoted from what he called an Australian Olympic anthem:

It's just not fair, but I don't care
As long as we beat New Zealand.

Together, New Zealand and Australia influenced rugby worldwide at times: from when, over many years, they wore down British opposition to replacements being allowed and to the kick into touch law, to most profoundly in the late 1980s with their force-fed introduction of a World Cup, and again in 1995 when they blasted away the British bedrock of rugby, amateurism.

Like any relationship, at times it has been warm and friendly, at other times a little distant and at still other times positively frosty. Sometimes it's been like a foundering marriage; the two partners have sometimes found it difficult to live together and just as difficult to live apart.

For a time, the two even considered becoming one or, rather, four becoming one. Late in the 19th century before Australia was a unified Commonwealth, the rugby bodies in the separate colonies of New Zealand, New South Wales, Queensland and Victoria considered amalgamation; all the better, they thought, to lobby for law changes at the remote (both geographically and mentally) Rugby Football Union in England, and to organise Antipodean tours by British sides.

It was ultimately the stand-alone success of the 1905 All Blacks that stilled such talk. Why merge with the others, was the argument, when we've proved on our own that we're equal to the best in the world?

But it was a lively topic as the rugby administrations in both countries developed and as the political leaders of the colonies on both sides of the Tasman talked of federation or, in New Zealand's case, talked of it as little as they could get away with.

The man regarded as the father of Australian federation, Henry Parkes, then the premier of New South Wales, met the New Zealand footballers in Sydney in 1893 — the first team chosen under the auspices of the New Zealand union — and told them 'the visits of athletic teams to the sister colonies must give rise to links of union and mutual respect'. It would be

NZ Rugby Museum

The 1893 team and officials in Australia before their opening match against Cumberland County at Parramatta.

impossible, Parkes said, for the New Zealanders to return home without having served the federation cause.

Within a week, the manager of the New Zealand team in Sydney, George Campbell, had raised the idea of one big union with New South Wales officials and in Wellington, the New Zealand union secretary, Ernest Hoben, said he would try to set up a trans-Tasman conference. (Campbell, incidentally, paid his own way as manager of the team, something subsequent managers could not have seen as a binding precedent.)

The whole thing went a formal stage further in October of 1893 when a meeting of resident delegates of the New Zealand union, that is, those who lived in Wellington, met and decided to recommend to the next annual meeting that it was 'advisable in the interests of rugby football that the Rugby Football Unions of the colonies should federate'. It listed 11 reasons for joining with their colonial brethren on the other side and Hoben was dispatched to Sydney to negotiate, even though an annual meeting had not had a chance to give its view.

Hoben had two meetings with New South Wales officials and spoke to what was described as a large gathering of the state's footballers and everyone, including delegates from Queensland and Victoria, thought it was a great idea. The Victorian union at the time was headed by a former Canterbury president, the Rev. John Hoatson, who had refereed one of the New Zealand games in Sydney.

The New Zealand union annual meeting in April of 1894 endorsed Hoben's actions and he told delegates that becoming one 'was a practical scheme to bind the unions together under one code of laws'.

Things did not move swiftly, though, even allowing for the fact that two-way communication between Wellington and Sydney took a couple of weeks other than expensive cabling, and that letters between Wellington and the various provincial unions could sometimes take as long.

At the next annual meeting, in 1895, delegates were told that New South Wales officials were preparing a draft constitution, but by the following year the issue seemed to have died. The next time it was mentioned in New Zealand union business was when Hoben, who by this time had left his unpaid job as founding secretary, wrote and said Queensland were still keen on an Australasian union.

They might have been, but they were even keener on playing host in 1899 to an England team chosen and managed by a colourful character, the Rev. Matthew Mullineaux. During the organisation of the tour, he wrote to New South Wales and said while he would love to play a New Zealand team, it would have to be somewhere in Australia because of a shortage of time.

Undeterred, New Zealand offered to pay the trans-Tasman costs of the team and pay the New South Wales union half the net proceeds taken in New Zealand. The rugby men in Sydney demurred, saying they needed a guaranteed payment of £500. When agreement couldn't be reached on this, New South Wales suggested a few New Zealanders cross the Tasman to make up an 'Australasian' team to play the English.

New Zealand wouldn't agree to that and there was a suspicion in New

Zealand that the Australians could have done more to extend the English tour. This was borne out in a letter from Sydney to Wellington:

> From private letters and rumours, of both of which we take little notice, it would appear that a feeling has gained strength in New Zealand that my union could have forced the Englishmen to visit New Zealand. I ask that you will contradict this, as there is absolutely too little time in their tour of four months to arrange any matches beyond Australia.

A kernel of simmering discontent could be detected in the final sentence of the letter: 'You can rest assured that my union is not likely in any way to be disloyal to yours.'

Players, as they can do, took matters into their own hands and the Sydney *Referee* said that New Zealand's decision not to send anyone to Sydney had the 'peculiar effect of causing several New Zealanders to come across on their own accord . . . no doubt some of them will show form sufficiently good to warrant their selection against England'.

The difficulty of arranging matches led to another move to form a combined Australasian union. This time its strongest and most active advocate was a former Wellington journalist, Charlie Marter, who was working in Sydney. (Marter had been a Wellington selector and was directly responsible for introducing Billy Wallace to rugby. Wallace related how the first football he handled as a child was one he and friends stole from Marter's house in Courtenay Place in Wellington. Years later, when Marter was a Wellington selector and Wallace a highly promising player, Wallace confessed to Marter. 'He laughed heartily,' Wallace recalled.)

The Sydney *Referee* reported:

> Marter has contrived to do a little football business of some importance to the game's future in his colony and in Australia. In New Zealand of late the formation of an Australasian Rugby Union has been discussed. The

NZ union has submitted the proposal to the local unions and there is little doubt that it will be adopted. Mr Marter has suggested to the New South Wales union the creation of such a body and . . . he thinks there will be no great difficulty in the way.

Joseph Firth, who had played for Nelson and Wellington and was soon to be appointed headmaster of Wellington College, moved at a special general meeting of the New Zealand union in May of 1899 that an Australasian union be formed 'to have entire control of the game in the Australasian colonies'. It lost by 21 votes to six. That was the end of that — for the time being.

Mullineaux's tour went ahead without any official New Zealand presence, although, as the Sydney *Referee* had predicted, four recent New Zealand arrivals played for Australia: Peter Ward, Walter Davis, Bill Hardcastle and Jum Sampson. To add to the New Zealand connection, the referee was 'Gun' Garrard of Christchurch, who, to the surprise of the genuine Australians, calmly fed scrums himself close to either side's line just to ensure a fair put-in. The series comprised Australia's first four tests — three in Sydney and one in Brisbane. Australia won the first but lost the rest. (Rev. Mullineaux did not disappear into rugby obscurity. He was proselytising in California when the First World War began and he took a ship to Wellington, where he signed up as an army chaplain. So, proving that God does indeed move in mysterious ways, rugby couldn't get Mullineaux to New Zealand but war could.)

Nothing further seems to have been done by any of the unions towards amalgamation but the idea still turned up from time to time in newspapers. The *Evening Post* suggested in 1901 that an annual Australasian rugby championship should be held and, two years later, a columnist in the *Canterbury Times* revived the idea of one combined union. This was supported by an unidentified writer in the *New Zealand Free Lance*, who said: 'It was never my idea that New Zealand footballers should live in a world of their own and an Australasian union would meet all requirements.'

New Zealand spanked Australia in its first test in Sydney in 1903 and the idea of joint strength waned even more. There were still diehards, as an editorial in the *Free Lance* indicated:

> Why not link closer to Australia? We don't want to federate in government, but we might federate in football. To send the part of a team to Australia to play in conjunction with the reps of the states against our British brothers would have helped along the friendly feeling we should have for our kin over the Tasman Sea.

All of this happened at a time of a web of trans-Tasman sporting contacts. In tennis, Anthony Wilding of New Zealand and Norman Brookes of Australia combined to win the Davis Cup three times for Australasia during the Edwardian era; the two countries fielded joint teams at the Olympic Games in 1908 and 1912; a New Zealand team played in the Australasian football (Aussie rules) carnival in Melbourne and nearly took All Black George Gillett with them; Australian Dally Messenger joined the first New Zealand league team on its tour of Britain in 1907 and in 1910, the Australian league team toured Britain and borrowed four New Zealanders. In athletics, joint New Zealand–Australian championship meetings were held until 1928.

(The joint Olympic teams raised the intriguing possibility of New Zealand being able to claim a share of the gold medal won in rugby by Australia in 1908, even though no New Zealanders were on the field. Technically, the team was an Australasian one, representing both countries and not just the bigger one.)

The gradual emergence from the amorphous collection of Australasian colonies into distinctive national identities brought an end to the talk of rugby sharing, and this was emphasised and consolidated by the success of the 1905–06 All Blacks in Britain and France. Thereafter, national teams became the fashion. The separate countries went their own ways with their own advantages and disadvantages and came together only when organising tours or when trying to lobby the English union or the International Rugby Board on law changes.

Those who dictated the shape of the rugby world from London had their own quaint ideas and when the New Zealand tour of Britain in 1924–25 was being organised, a suggestion was made at a meeting of the English union that New South Wales players should be included in the team and that it should be called 'Anzac'. The New Zealand union had a representative on that union, Cecil Wray, and he made it very plain that as revered a name as Anzac was for both countries, there would be no joint team.

Years later, there was. The final match of the British Isles' tour of Australia in 1989 was at Ballymore against 'an Anzac Selection'. The original selection had seven New Zealanders and eight Australians in it but by the time the teams took the field, there were only three All Blacks — Steve McDowell at prop, Frano Botica in the midfield and Kieran Crowley at fullback.

The Anzac idea had come up a couple of times during the New South Wales tour of New Zealand in 1923 when preliminary plans were being made for the 1924 British tour. The New South Wales manager, Harry Bosward, said at the dinner after the first 'test' in Dunedin the team for Britain should be a combined one, but the chairman of the New Zealand union, Stan Dean, was firmly opposed. 'New Zealand is proud of her footballers and football honours and only a New Zealand team should go Home and would be pleased to meet Australia in Blighty,' he said.

Later, on the eve of New South Wales going home, Dean returned to the Anzac idea:

I don't think the proposal was very popular either in Australia or New Zealand. Both are now able to stand on their own footing in the football and athletics world and if we are victorious, the added glory will be ours just the same as the additional merit will be Australia's if the blue riband comes her way. Both have got past the swaddling clothes stage and there is an individuality and an independence which it would be foolish indeed to weaken.

Rugby had collapsed in Queensland after the First World War and New South Wales alone carried the rugby banner, which was why the All Blacks played New South Wales during the 1920s and not Australia. These matches were given retrospective test status by the Australian union in 1988 but the New Zealand union, periodically asked for its views, has steadfastly maintained that test status is for matches against national, not state, sides. (Despite this, current administrators may be dismayed to learn, the New Zealand union decided in 1901 to award caps to those who played against New South Wales that year.)

Relations once Queensland was reformed were cordial more often than not — at least off the field — and New Zealand acknowledged that Australia had a unique problem: rugby was not the dominant sport it was in New Zealand. Victorian rugby had faded almost to extinction under the weight of Australian rules (now AFL) and the game barely existed in the other rules states of Tasmania, South Australia and Western Australia. In Queensland and New South Wales, particularly the latter, rugby league developed enormously after the First World War and for most of the rest of the century, Australian rugby — 'the rah-rah boys' — lived at times almost a hand to mouth existence. Star players leaving amateur rugby for semi-professional league became a fact of sporting life from the early 1960s on.

There is what could be described as an urban myth, not supported by any found evidence, that New Zealand rugby on at least two occasions helped Australian rugby out of financial holes, quite separate from generating gate money. New Zealand's willingness to host state tours, especially from the 1960s on, also gave Australian rugby players a greater experience and a wider horizon than they would otherwise have had. When the Australian team led by a New Zealander, Greg Davis, toured New Zealand in 1972, it was derided for its inability to compete with the All Blacks (or even the provinces). Its coach, Bob Templeton, frankly remarked that if it were not for New Zealand, Australian rugby would be in an even more parlous state.

There were still family spats. One of the Australian delegates to an

International Rugby Board meeting in London in 1968, Wylie Breckenridge, was fiercely critical of New Zealand both at the meeting and later socially. He apparently had a track record for speaking first and thinking later (if at all) but enough seemed to be enough for the New Zealanders in 1968. The chairman of the New Zealand union, Tom Morrison, wrote a letter of complaint to his Australian counterpart, Charles Blunt.

Ron Palenski Collection

A New Zealander who captained Australia: Greg Davis.

'Breck went out of his way to be critical of New Zealand, not only in informal company, but during the actual IRB meeting,' Morrison wrote. While others praised the All Blacks for their play in Britain in 1967, Breckenridge evidently made comments along the lines of, 'Wait until they go to South Africa in 1970, they will revert to the old game of kick, kick, kick.' He also said it was time New Zealand woke up as to who its friends were — an apparent reference to New Zealand being dismissive of Australia while toadying to the dominant British unions.

'I have been prepared to turn a deaf ear to his carping outbursts,' Morrison wrote, 'but I feel I must tell you . . . that Breck's attitude to New Zealand could cause harm to the excellent spirit that exists between us.'

Blunt, in a masterly diplomatic reply, said: 'Breck can be undiplomatic at times but you must not take his remarks too seriously. I know that in his heart he shares the same affection for New Zealand as I do.'

Ron Palenski Collection

Ces Blazey, who had some blunt words for Australia.

Ces Blazey, who was one of the New Zealand delegates in London, also wrote to Blunt and said he was thoroughly tired of the tenor of Breckenridge's remarks:

Quite frankly, there is a limit to how much we should be expected to tolerate . . . when the criticism of New Zealand is unprovoked . . . I think we were well beyond the toleration point this year when the last of several critical comments warned that New Zealand would be well advised to consider where she would need friends in the future and 'they are not on this side of the world'. I was sorely tempted to reply forthwith but a look at the faces of most of the other delegates made me decide to treat it with the contempt which it deserves.

That spat was kept in-house but other disagreements between New Zealand and Australia have not been. Two of the most celebrated — if that is the right word — were of recent vintage. Both involved the World Cup which, ironically, the two countries launched with barely a strained word between them. Not so when the cup had taken off to become such a money-making venture.

New Zealand's loss of the sub-hosting rights to the 2003 cup were the cause of some terse trans-Tasman exchanges (and between Wellington and London as well). That disagreement came in the context of relations already strained because of New Zealand's continued refusal — at the time — to expand the Super 12 by two teams. In fact, the two issues ran side by side for a while. At one point, the chief executive of the Australian union, John O'Neill, accused the New Zealand union of 'obfuscation and lack of realism' and warned of the possibility of significant damage to the relationship between the two unions.

The cup was the catalyst for another falling out in 2005 when the Australians — with O'Neill away running soccer at the time — favoured Japan ahead of New Zealand to stage the 2011 cup. The two men who headed the successful New Zealand bid, Jock Hobbs and Chris Moller, left little doubt about what they thought of their mates on the other side.

Since Victorian days as colonies, New Zealanders and Australians have got along as neighbours more often than they have not. Isolated geographically in a rugby world dominated from Europe, the two have usually realised each is important to the other. As an old Qantas commercial once had it, 'They're our old friends from over the sea.'

'Ernest' Endeavours Founded Union

For a sporting body that has seemed over the years to have spent as much time courting journalists as it has cursing them, it seems richly ironic that the New Zealand Rugby Union was founded by a reporter.

Ernest Denis Hoben mounted almost a lone crusade in the last decade of the 19th century to bring some semblance of national unity and order to the scattered provincial unions which were by no means initially convinced of the need for a central, national body.

He once argued:

> The position I have taken up has been the result of rubbing shoulders with rugby union men all over the colony, and finding everywhere the same grievance and wants, and the same desire for a practical solution of the difficulties by the formation of a union whose work would begin where that of existing unions must perforce leave off.

The rugbyscape in 19th-century New Zealand was vastly different from what it is now. While the provincial unions had largely taken the geographical shape they still retain, there was only limited contact between them because of rudimentary communications and transport. Some unions were affiliated to the English governing body, the Rugby Football Union, which acted then in rugby in much the same overarching way internationally as the MCC did for many years in cricket. If there were a dispute about playing laws, some unions would determine the outcome for themselves; others would appeal to London for resolution.

Until Hoben came along, a truly national rugby team was not possible. A New Zealand Native team, it is true, toured Britain and Australia in 1888–89 and a national team went to New South Wales in 1884, but both were organised by private promoters and neither could be said to be wholly representative of the strength of New Zealand rugby.

Until Hoben, New Zealand rugby could not speak with one voice.

Hoben was just 28 — young for rugby administrators then or now — when provincial unions got together at the Club Hotel in Wellington on April 16, 1892 and formed the New Zealand union.

The *Otago Witness* derided Hoben as being alone in having a burning desire to see the formation of a national body. He denied that, but a summary of his active life to that point seems to indicate a burning desire to get things done.

Hoben was born in Auckland but spent his boyhood in Tauranga where it was written he 'had quite a local reputation by reason of his participation in various athletic games, chess and literary clubs, and as a cross-country walker, a long-distance runner, a boxer and, in fact, he was captain or chief officer of nearly all the local organisations.' He played rugby for Tauranga — and was said to be a speedy wing threequarter — at a time of annual matches with Auckland.

While still a teenager and working for the Bank of New Zealand, he and Edward Mortimer Edgcumbe, a nephew of the Earl of Edgcumbe, started a daily newspaper, the *Tauranga Telegraph*, which had but a brief existence.

Hoben moved on to Hawke's Bay where he became secretary of the Hawke's Bay Rugby Union and, according to one report, 'brought that body into prominence and helped to make football the great pastime of the Bay, among the Maoris as well as the Europeans'.

It was while working and playing in Hawke's Bay that he began to formulate his ideas for a national union. His secretarial duties gave him some opportunity for travel but he was also fortunate that he could accompany his older brother Sydney, a concert pianist who had trained at the Royal Conservatorium in Leipzig in Germany, on a tour of New Zealand.

For all his rugby and tripping around, Hoben continued as a keen tramper and was once, in October of 1891, feared lost in rugged bush country in the Ruahine Range. He managed to find his way out as a search party was finding its way in.

Within a month of that escapade, he convened a meeting in Wellington that led to the formation of the New Zealand union. As Arthur Swan noted in his history of New Zealand rugby:

> Mr Hoben spent a considerable amount of his time during 1891 touring through the Colony putting his idea of a New Zealand Union before the various local Unions, explaining the proposed working of such a Union and the benefits to be obtained by have the headquarters of the Game in New Zealand.

The only objections were from Otago and Canterbury. Otago, which argued a national union was premature and that provincial unions already had the power of English county unions, nevertheless attended the initial meeting on November 7 in Wellington. Canterbury did not bother, saying it would wait until its officials had read the proposed constitution.

Hoben outlined to the two-day meeting why he thought a national union was necessary and what reactions he had received from the provincial unions and at the end of the two days, the delegates voted in favour. Hoben was elected the first secretary.

In the week after the conference, the *Otago Witness* published, under the name of 'Forward' (rugby administrator and journalist James Hutchison) a lengthy criticism of Hoben's ideal, repeating the arguments previously mounted that it was premature and complaining that Otago did not want to be governed by Wellington men (Canterbury had a similar objection).

Hoben responded to the criticisms, saying Otago would need to make up its mind for isolation or co-operation before the date set for the founding meeting, April 16, 1892. 'Of the need for a central governing body I think it unnecessary for me to speak,' he said.

NZ Rugby Museum

Rowing, athletics, racing, tennis, bowling, yachting, all have their associations and all have benefited therefrom. Even Association football, which so far as New Zealand is concerned is a thing of yesterday, and affecting, as compared to Rugby, but a handful of players, has its central union in good working order, and which has given a strong impetus to

Ernest Hoben, the journalist whose endeavours led to the formation of the New Zealand union.

the development of the game. Rugby football is undoubtedly the national winter pastime of New Zealand and yet, so far, is the only sport which has not accepted the benefits of national co-operation.

Otago and Canterbury's objections notwithstanding (and they were joined by Southland), the union was formed at the April 1892 meeting and Hoben was confirmed as its first secretary. (The effect of the three unions staying out was they were barred from playing anyone but each other and the first national team under the NZRFU was selected in the following year without any consideration of Otago, Canterbury or Southland players. All three fell into line and joined the union by 1895.)

Hoben was an unpaid, voluntary secretary and when not involved in rugby business, he continued as a journalist. He moved to Wellington and became a reporter on the *Evening Post*, working in the parliamentary press gallery as well as being a music and drama critic. He gained something of a reputation as a journalist who 'broke' stories and was even the subject of a royal commission that tried to establish how Hoben was able to acquire and write about correspondence between the commandant of the New Zealand military, Francis Fox, and the Premier, Richard Seddon. The correspondence included Fox's resignation and a catalogue of complaints about Seddon. Both Hoben and his editor, Edward Gillon, refused to appear before the commission.

In conjunction with his brother, Hoben also wrote songs which apparently were received favourably (including one called 'Cromaboo' which had a rugby theme); he wrote poetry and a pamphlet on the life of the Liberal premier, John Ballance, which apparently was published to acclaim in New Zealand and in Britain.

Hoben left the New Zealand union and Wellington in January of 1896 to take up a job on the *Daily Telegraph* in Sydney and he later became assistant editor of the *Sydney Mail*.

He returned to New Zealand in 1906 after his wife died (he had met her while she was a nurse at Wellington Hospital) and took over as manager of the weekly *New Zealand Times*, until he bought the lease for the *Manawatu Times*, which he ran for four years. He returned to Australia for a stint on the *Sydney Morning Herald* before moving to the *Herald and Weekly Times* in Melbourne. He died on his birthday, February 3, in 1918, apparently in the presence of a close friend, William McKenzie.

Little was known about Hoben's last years, or indeed, where he was buried, until 2001 when his descendants, with the help of the Victorian Rugby Union, found his grave in a suburban Melbourne cemetery.

The New Zealand union, at the urging of the family, happily paid for the grave to be repaired and be given a modern headstone that bears the silver fern. This prompted a flurry of interest in Hoben by people who had otherwise never heard of him and a *Sydney Morning Herald* writer, Roy Masters, reprinted parts of an obituary written by McKenzie.

Masters doesn't say so, but the McKenzie who was present at Hoben's death and who wrote the obituary was surely 'Offside Mac' McKenzie, an All Black wing forward in the 1890s who gained his nickname for obvious reasons. McKenzie, like Hoben, was also a journalist and lived his later life in Melbourne, where he died in 1943.

McKenzie also wrote to Hoben's oldest son, Duncan, in Sydney and related how he recalled seeing Hoben 'striding down Lambton Quay in company with Richard Seddon — two men at that time carrying all before them by means of persistent application and all-round ability'.

The New Zealand union, having rediscovered its founder, now has at its Wellington headquarters an Ernest Hoben Room in his honour.

The Dream Test Run

For a shade over three years from the time the All Blacks won the first World Cup, they were undeniably and emphatically the best team in the world. They may not have been unbeatable, but no one could beat them.

Australia tried seven times, Wales four, France, Scotland and Argentina three each and Ireland, Italy and Fiji each had one crack. England did not play the All Blacks at all during that period and South Africa was then off the international scene because of its apartheid policy.

Between May 22, 1987 and August 18, 1990, New Zealand went through a record 23 test matches unbeaten, with a draw against Australia the only smudge on the ledger. No other All Black team has been so successful for so long. The streak was six matches better than the 17 test victories between 1965 and 1970 (although that side did have a draw against East Wales in 1967).

As was the pattern at the time, and as it had been since the first tour, the All Blacks of 1987–90 also played midweek and Saturday matches against non-test opposition. There were 27 of those matches and all were won. So the All Blacks of 1987–90 went 50 matches without a loss.

In the 23 test matches that passed by without defeat, the All Blacks scored 488 points; their opponents 257, roughly half. The All Blacks scored 86 tries, an average of nearly four a match, and their opponents just 25.

Remarkably, and even more remarkable today in an era of substitutes and rotation, the All Blacks achieved their streak by using just 32 players — and four of them played just one match each and another seven played five or fewer.

Three of the streak team played in every one of the matches: lock Gary Whetton (captain for the last two), first five-eighths Grant Fox and hooker Sean Fitzpatrick. One player, prop Steve McDowell, missed just one of the 23. Another three players, wing John Kirwan, centre Joe Stanley and flanker Alan Whetton, played in 21 of the matches.

It was an era of sustained excellence by the All Blacks, an era unmatched in New Zealand rugby. Yet it ended, as all eras ultimately do for one reason or another.

The beginning of the era is easy to pinpoint. It was the first game of the first World Cup when New Zealand beat Italy 70–6 and Kirwan ignited the tournament with his end-to-end try.

The end of the era is less easy to pin down. Statistically, it ended at Athletic Park in Wellington on August 18, 1990 when Australia won 21–9. That was the third of a series of three tests and the All Blacks won the series — had already won it before they went to Wellington. Later in 1990 substantially the same team beat France in two tests and, the following year, beat Argentina in two tests and then shared a two-test series with Australia (a home win each). The second World Cup came after that: the All Blacks beat England, the United States, Italy and, in a quarter-final, Canada before losing the semi-final to Australia in Dublin.

Statistically, the era was already at an end; Dublin was the emotional finale. It was the end of the line for the team that set new rugby standards in the first World Cup and all but carried them through to the second. At the start of the era, the All Blacks were enthusiastic, innovative, creative, exciting. By the end, they looked care-worn, their play looked repetitive, some players looked as if they had hung on too long, and, perhaps worst of all, they were roundly criticised for being arrogant — a return to the 'unsmiling giants' tag of earlier tours.

One of the men there throughout the era, Grant Fox, thought the era really ended in Dublin. 'To my mind, the real match-play championship was in Dublin for it was there on the world stage that the Wallabies snuffed out the All Black candle,' he wrote.

Fox also agreed with the 'arrogant' tag, though did not do so at the time it was being levelled. In a speech he delivers about his years as an All Black at dinners and other social occasions, he acknowledges the All Blacks collectively were arrogant or, at least, could certainly be seen to be so. The players did not agree with the accusations at the time, and felt hurt by them, but Fox concedes now they were an arrogant team.

Dublin as an endpoint to the era is also lent credence because the World Cup in 1991 was the last time Alex Wyllie was there as coach, or co-coach as it happened. Wyllie and his co-coach in 1991, John Hart, had begun the era as assistants to coach Brian Lochore in 1987. The coaching musical chairs resulted in Hart taking the team to Japan later in 1987 with Wyllie as his assistant, and then Wyllie being given sole charge from 1988 on. Wyllie, Lane Penn and Earle Kirton were the selectors in 1988 and Hart rejoined the panel in place of Kirton in 1989 and was made co-coach with Wyllie for the 1991 World Cup. The era team was, to all intents and purposes, Wyllie's team.

While all good things must inevitably come to an end, what went wrong? How could the team that was the best in the world slip so soon to being, on the basis of the 1991 cup results, the third best? How could a team that dominated world rugby so suddenly become just another team in the pack? The All Blacks these days are sometimes derided for being the best team between World Cups. If that jibe is true, and evidence lends it credibility, it was the 1991 team that began that unfortunate trend.

The cumulative effect of several decisions finally caught up with the All Blacks in Dublin. It wasn't any one or two or even three of the decisions on their own; or even decisions made by selectors or the players on the field. Some of the decisions had been made the year before or even the year before that. But it was the coming together of the results of those decisions that led first of all to a loss of authority by the All Blacks and then, finally and crucially, to the defeat by Australia at Lansdowne Road.

One decision was that made by the fullback, John Gallagher, to take up a league contract in England. His departure in 1990 affected the balance

Ron Palenski Collection

John Gallagher, whose loss was sorely felt by the All Blacks.

and the pattern of the style of play on which the successful era had been predicated. He was the most attacking fullback the All Blacks had had since Bob Scott in the late 1940s and early 1950s. His manner of play was ideally fitted to the All Black philosophy as laid out by Lochore, Hart and Wyllie when the cup squad first got together in 1987.

Losing the popular 'Kipper' to an offer he could not refuse was one factor. But he had led indirectly to the loss of his earmarked replacement, Matthew Ridge. Ridge had been on the tour of Wales and Ireland in 1989 and was clearly seen as a test fullback of the future, but he felt that his path was blocked by Gallagher. When he received an offer from Sydney rugby league team Manly, he went. He made his decision public after Gallagher had negotiated with Leeds but before Gallagher said anything publicly. Gallagher admitted he was stunned by Ridge's news and wondered if he should have let Ridge know what he was planning, or somehow dropped a hint. But it was too late to wonder. The incumbent test fullback and the heir presumptive fullback were both lost to the All Blacks.

The transfer of the pair to league was big news at the time. At that stage of rugby's gradual weaning off the burden of amateurism, there was no way back for either of them. They were, as older rugby people used to say, beyond the pale. They were gone. Other All Blacks went to league in 1990, their departure perhaps hastened by the International Rugby Board's refusal at its annual meeting in March of that year to countenance any relaxation of the straitjacket amateurism regulations.

Gallagher's great mate from Wellington, John Schuster, also went, as did Grant Fox's perennial back-up, Frano Botica, and the Waikato pair of Paul Simonsson and Daryl Halligan, the first of them briefly an All Black in 1987 and the second perhaps an All Black of the future.

Overshadowing even the moves to league in the big news stakes was the decision by Wyllie to drop Wayne Shelford, captain since the tour of Japan in late 1987. The talismanic Shelford was virtually the epitome of the All Blacks or, at least, of the image the rugby public has of the All Blacks. Unquestionably hard and uncompromising, the classic leader by example, Shelford was the type who put team ahead of self. There were a few comments around during Shelford's All Black career that if you had to pick one All Black to be by your side in the trenches or in a tough spot in the Western Desert, Shelford would be the one.

Most New Zealanders knew the story of how against France in Nantes Shelford's scrotum was almost ripped off; it made men's eyes water with a mixture of admiration at Shelford's attitude to pain and imagination of it happening to themselves. Trained in the navy, Shelford knew what a crucial role discipline played in a group of disparate young men. He would enforce it if necessary. On the field, he never hesitated to right wrongs: the punch that sent Huw Richards of Wales into oblivion in 1987 was only the most public of his instant judgments.

Off the field, Shelford had a commanding presence; there was never any doubt who the captain was. Suffering fools did not come naturally to him, but he did his best in those innumerable beyond-rugby tasks that befall an All Black captain.

Peter Bush

The winning captain and resuscitator of the haka, Wayne Shelford.

He was also the living embodiment of the resurrection of the haka from 1987, performing it proudly and correctly and ensuring his team-mates did the same, rather than the offhand uncoordinated and self-conscious jiggling around it had been previously. The sole rehearsal of the haka for players of earlier eras was usually gyrating around in a hotel room the morning of the match. Shelford brought choreography and mana to it.

The outrage when he was dropped was genuine and widespread, exacerbated by the weird tales and rumours which followed it. One supposed story centred on a dust-up he, Fox and Wyllie had in a dressing room. Anyone who knew Fox, Shelford and Wyllie knew what a flight of fancy that was. And even if it were true, it would not have been difficult to pick the odd man out.

Shelford's omission led to the amazing phenomenon of the spontaneous 'Bring Back Buck' campaign, surely the loudest and longest reaction to the dropping of any All Black at any time. 'Bring Back Buck' became a phrase embedded in the New Zealand sporting lexicon and signs bearing the legend still pop up at the unlikeliest of places, the Australian and United States Open tennis tournaments among the more bizarre.

Buck was never brought back, although he did captain a second New Zealand team against New Zealand Universities, Romania and the Soviet Union in 1991. It says much for Shelford's character that he deigned even to accept selection in such a comedown team.

So by the end of June in 1990, the All Black team on an unprecedented string of unbeaten matches was already taking on a much different shape. The signs of greatness were starting to slip away. They nearly lost to Scotland for the first time, only Grant Fox's goal-kicking keeping the unblemished record. The Scots in the second test in Auckland scored two tries to one and could justly claim to have been the better side but Fox's kicking, and a curious penalty against the Scottish fullback, Gavin Hastings, which Fox turned into another three points, were the decisive factors. That was Shelford's last test.

There had been idle speculation around the fringes of the team for some time that Wyllie was increasingly worried about Shelford's form; that he was no longer the commanding presence that he once was. Had there not been a ready replacement, Shelford's execution may have been stayed. But Zinzan Brooke, who at that stage had played two tests as a flanker (the second of them as a replacement), had long been regarded as the future All Black No. 8. It was a straightforward matter, at least in selection terms, to put him in for Shelford. Of course, it wasn't straightforward in any other terms.

A new captain had to be found as well as a No. 8. Gary Whetton was chosen because of his seniority — he first played a test in 1981 — and the not inconsequential fact he was an automatic selection for every test team. He was a leader by dint of his size, his presence on the field and his influence, especially among the Aucklanders, off it. But captaincy did not sit lightly on those broad shoulders. On the field he may have been fine, but off it he did not have the easy authority that marks out the better captains. That was another decision that would have a direct bearing on the performance of the All Blacks in 1991.

A hallmark of the Wyllie era team was its consistency in selection. Wyllie, whatever else his critics said of him, was loyal to his players and he seemed reluctant to change unless change was forced upon him such as injury. That made the Shelford sacking even more surprising.

The team that played in the match that ended the streak, the loss to Australia in 1990, was starting to look different from the team that had won the World Cup and sustained the All Blacks through 1988 and 1989. Kieran Crowley was at fullback in place of Gallagher, Terry Wright on a wing in place of Craig Green who had gone to Italy, Craig Innes was at centre for Joe Stanley and Walter Little at second five-eighths for the retired Warwick Taylor. Graeme Bachop was at fullback instead of Bruce Deans, who had taken over from David Kirk. Mike Brewer, who would have been in the 1987 cup squad instead of Brooke but for injury, was on the openside flank instead of Michael Jones, whose knee ligaments had been smashed the year before against Argentina. Ian Jones was in his first year of test rugby, having taken over from Murray Pierce, who had retired.

Ron Palenski Collection

Joe Stanley shows the qualities which could have benefited the All Blacks in 1991.

All of those players, though, had been in or about the All Blacks for the past few years, Innes, Little and Jones being blooded on the tour of Wales and Ireland in 1989.

When the Wallabies won the third test in Wellington, it was the first defeat in black for Wyllie. There were comments at the time that the loss could prove to be beneficial in terms of the World Cup the following year. Such woolly thinking does not sit well with All Blacks or those concerned about the record fashioned over nearly a hundred years. The only possible benefit from a loss would be if it exposed deficiencies in a team that might otherwise not have been exposed and changes could then be made. But changes were not made and the team that went to France late in 1990 and won both tests was still substantially the same that Wyllie had created.

It was around this time that the New Zealand Rugby Union put together a committee aimed at seeing everything possible was done to ensure the All Blacks retained the World Cup. No expense was to be spared. The All Blacks want a fitness trainer? Give them one. They want to fly business class so they arrive fresher than if they had travelled economy? Of course. Better training aids, more clothing? Anything.

Well, not quite anything. The New Zealand union still decided what games should be played and the All Blacks were dispatched to Argentina in 1991 on a nine-match tour of dubious benefit, especially for the key man in the backs, Fox.

Back on this side of the Pacific, the All Blacks played two Bledisloe Cup tests, one in Sydney that was lost and the other in Auckland that was won 6–3. Both matches showed that the Australians were a team on the rise; the All Blacks, if not in decline, were on a plateau. In their last three meetings, the Australians had won twice and the New Zealanders once, and even that was hardly convincing. It looked incongruous when Gary Whetton happily hoisted the Bledisloe Cup aloft at Eden Park.

Injuries in 1991 played a key role in the emotional end of the era. Not so much injuries *per se*, because they are endemic to any elite group of athletes, but how they were dealt with. Fox, for example, suffered a pelvic injury in Argentina and painkilling injections were added to his pre-match ritual for the rest of the year. The imperative to keep Fox playing showed his value to the team, but was that the wisest option? Perhaps if he had stopped playing for Auckland, been left out of the two pre-cup tests against Australia and even missed the opening rounds of cup matches, he might have been fully fit when it really mattered. But that is conjecture. It didn't happen that way. He continued to play and in the semi-final against Australia, when a try-saving tackle on David Campese needed to be made, Fox couldn't make it.

It did not escape Fox's notice that had he been medically tested as thoroughly before the cup as Mike Brewer was, he may not have been at the cup at all. Brewer, in one of the more controversial decisions that affected the end of the era, was declared unfit for the cup campaign yet within a week or so was playing spectacularly for Otago. Fox, as he himself noted, passed his medical after declaring what his injury was.

The decision by Gallagher to go to Leeds had a long-term effect at the cup. Wyllie had not been able to settle on a replacement. Crowley was tried but not included in the cup squad. Terry Wright, a wing with blistering pace, became the cup fullback and when he was injured, John Timu — another who was introduced to the All Blacks in 1989 — was tried there in the quarter-final against Canada. Wyllie and Hart thought of calling for the Otago fullback, Greg Cooper, who they thought was in Italy. But he wasn't so they sent for Crowley as a replacement instead. But Crowley, for all his experience and admirable qualities as a fullback, did not have the speed that Wright had and the All Blacks therefore had to rethink their strategy to attack out wide, utilising the pace of wings and fullback.

Another decision that may have had an effect on the result in Dublin was made many years before. It was the decision by the freakishly gifted loose forward, Michael Jones, not to play on Sundays. There was the occasional critic in New Zealand who held the view that no player, including Jones, should be able to pick and choose which tests to be available for. Jones had such extraordinary gifts that coaches were just grateful they could have him some of the time. The cup semi-final against Australia was not one of those times.

Would he have made a difference? It's impossible to know but on the basis that he tended to make a substantial difference in most games he played, the outcome in Dublin could well have been different. His importance to the team was stressed by one supporter who told him before the semi-final: 'If you think about it Michael, the game is actually being played Monday morning in New Zealand so you could play.'

The match was lost, the era that ended statistically the year before had now ended emotionally. The All Blacks beat Scotland in the play-off match and so finished third in the cup, but that was no consolation for either the team or for New Zealand. All Blacks don't play for bronze medals.

It was the end for Wyllie, despite his excellent record as a coach, and the end for several of the players, including the captain, Gary Whetton, and his brother, Alan. It was a temporary end for John Hart as well, cast aside until after the next World Cup. And as the rugby world developed because of the impetus of the cup, and as it moved rapidly toward inevitable professionalism, 1991 may also have marked the beginning of the end of the All Black aura. Still difficult to beat of course, but not unbeatable. Other teams used to fear the All Blacks; but the fear became simple respect.

PLAYERS OF THE ERA
(possible 23 tests from May 22, 1987 until August 18, 1990):

23   Sean Fitzpatrick, Grant Fox, Gary Whetton.

22   Steve McDowell.

21   John Kirwan, Joe Stanley, Alan Whetton.

20   Wayne Shelford.

18   John Gallagher, Richard Loe, Murray Pierce.

17   Terry Wright.

13   Michael Jones.

10   Bruce Deans, John Schuster.

8   Mike Brewer, Warwick Taylor.

7   David Kirk.

6   Graeme Bachop, John Drake, Craig Green.

5   Kieran Crowley, Bernie McCahill.

4   Zinzan Brooke, Craig Innes, Ian Jones, Walter Little.

3   Andy Earl.

1   Albert Anderson, Frano Botica, Mark
     Brooke-Cowden, Kevin Schuler.

			t	c	p	dg	total	t	c	p	dg	total
	UNBEATEN TEST STREAK												
				New Zealand						Opposition					
1	1987	Italy	12	8	2		70			1	1	6
2		Fiji	12	10	2		74	1		3		13
3		Argentina	6	2	6		46	1	1	3		15
4		Scotland	2	2	6		30			1		3
5		Wales	8	7	1		49	1	1			6
6		France	3	1	4	1	29	1	1	1		9
7		Australia	4	1	3	1	30	1		3	1	16
8	1988	Wales	10	6			52			1		3
9		Wales	8	8	2		54	1	1	1		9
10		Australia	5	3	2		32	1		1		7
11		Australia	3	2	1		19	2	1	3		19
12		Australia	3	3	4		30	1	1	1		9
13	1989	France	3	2	3		25	3	1	1		17
14		France	4	3	4		34	2		4		20
15		Argentina	10	7	2		60	1	1	1		9
16		Argentina	7	6	3		49	1	1	2		12
17		Australia	2	2	4		24	1	1	2		12
18		Wales	4	3	4		34			3		9
19		Ireland	3	1	3		23			2		6
20	1990	Scotland	5	4	1		31	3	2			16
21		Scotland	1	1	5		21	2	2	2		18
22		Australia	4	1	1		21			2		6
23		Australia	3	3	2	1	27	2		2	1	17
Totals			122	86	65	3	864	25	14	40	3	257
Points per			x4	x2	x3	x3		x4	x2	x3	x3	
Total Points			488	172	195	9	864	100	28	120	9	257

Birth of the World Cup

Strange as it may seem, the World Cup was introduced to the rugby world with the purist aim of keeping the game amateur; as a means of keeping the charging forces of professionalism at bay. It had — and this prospect could not have gone unnoticed at the time — the complete opposite effect.

The World Cup was the thin end of the wedge that drove apart the reactionaries, mainly in Britain and Ireland, who did not want the game sullied by money (unless they earned it themselves, of course), and the visionaries, who saw the wider world development of rugby as crucial to its survival.

The International Rugby Board, dominated by the three British unions and Ireland, had long resisted any form of international tournament, although they were happy enough to reap the benefits of their own, the Five Nations (which is now Six). It was the classic amateur position: the game was the thing; it was for the gentlemen players, not for spectators.

The idea of a World Cup, or an international rose by any other name, had been around for a long time and every time its head was propped up above the parapet, it was shot down.

Initial suggestions for an international tournament came from continental Europe, which the IRB regarded with a great deal of suspicion and disdain. Across the English Channel, the prevailing view held, was a hotbed of nascent professionalism and other undesirable practices.

The board ignored as best it could tournaments which were held in Berlin in 1936 (France, Italy, Germany and Romania) and in 1937 in Paris (France,

107

One of the rugby posters produced for the last time the game was played at the Olympics, in Paris in 1924.

Italy, Germany, Romania, Belgium and Holland). The Berlin tournament was held in conjunction with the Olympic Games there (though not a part of the Olympics, from which rugby disappeared in 1924). New Zealand flirted briefly, incidentally, with sending a team to the 1924 Olympics but dropped the idea presumably because of opposition from their tour hosts that year, England.

In 1933, Italy proposed an international federation of all rugby-playing countries and not just the white, English-speaking ones. An official history of the IRB up until 1960 recorded haughtily and insultingly: 'The invitation went on to beg the sister federations to report their views, so that the ITALIANS might arrange for "a congress of the European federations to discuss . . . and proceed . . ."!' (The capitals and exclamation mark were the IRB's.)

The Italians were at it again when they were able to re-establish their rugby after the Second World War. They suggested to the IRB that it support a rugby tournament in Rome in 1960 to coincide with the Olympic Games. Again, the IRB's sub-text was plain when it recorded: 'The board refused its support and it is noteworthy that in 1959 some 23 of the leading Italian clubs were reported to have combined to form a professional rugby competition.'

By this time, the board had a regulation on its books: 'No approval can be given to participation by teams from Member Unions in any competition or tournament, at whatever level or wherever taking place, in which teams from several countries take part.' (Member unions were then England, Scotland, Wales, Ireland, New Zealand, Australia and South Africa. France was not admitted to rugby's inner sanctum until 1978 and others not until 1987.)

Even the Five Nations was not sanctioned by the British and Irish unions as a formal event. As far as the Home Nations (as they liked to call themselves) were concerned, the January–February matches each year were 'friendlies' and not interconnected. Points tables and descriptors such as 'triple crown' and 'grand slam' were, as far as the denizens of the rugby deep were concerned, the creations of newspapers. It was only in 1993, six years after the first World Cup, that the tournament was officially recognised.

Greater forces were at work, though, preparing to drag rugby out of its 19th century Corinthian cocoon. Increasing commercialism, aided and abetted by rapidly developing communications networks which sped and spread the process of globalisation, gradually transformed the face of international sport. If the British could not see this happening, New Zealanders and Australians could.

There has been some debate about who from within rugby first suggested a World Cup. Gerald Davies, the great Welsh wing who wrote a history of the cup in 2003, said the president of the Australian Rugby Union, Bill McLaughlin, had first contemplated the idea in 1979.

Another cup historian and former player, Derek Wyatt, also went for McLaughlin, although he quoted Nick Shehadie, who played a leading role in the organisation of the first cup, as saying the real cup credit should go to an earlier Australian, Harold Tolhurst, a Wallaby test wing who had toured New Zealand in 1931 and refereed tests against New Zealand in 1951.

Ces Blazey of New Zealand, regarded in his time as one of the best administrators the game had seen, also raised the cup idea in 1979. Recalling an IRB meeting that year, he recorded: 'We raised the question of the possibility of the board being interested in a World Cup-type competition although we were aware of the historic opposition of the board. The idea found no support.'

Blazey did not specify who comprised the 'we' and while it was likely he was referring to New Zealand's other delegate to the meeting, Bob Stuart, he could equally have been referring to McLaughlin.

(As an indication of Blazey's worth and influence, at the same meeting he successfully persuaded the IRB board to allow touch judges, by means of a raised flag, to advise referees of foul play. He also sought the introduction of temporary suspension but the sin bin was then a step too far for his international colleagues.)

It wasn't just the global forces approaching rugby's gates. So too were players. Graham Mourie retired from international rugby in 1982 and wrote a book (declaring himself a professional for doing so) in which he wrote the IRB was in danger of finding itself a head without a body. He said sanity and reality had to be introduced to the rugby world, ideally by the IRB making itself a truly international body but 'at the very least, to organise some form of competition which would allow the smaller rugby nations to compete against the big league'.

In the same year, a London sports promoter and television host, Neil Durden-Smith, took a plan for a cup to the IRB. Not unexpectedly, it was rejected but it was at least another indication to the board of what was wanted in the real world. (Durden-Smith was familiar with New Zealand rugby, having served as a naval officer as an aide-de-camp to a New Zealand Governor-General, Lord Cobham.) One of the reasons given for the rejection of Durden-Smith's plan was that his cup would have been controlled by a private company and not by the IRB. A former English president of the international soccer body, FIFA, Sir Stanley Rous, was frequently quoted during cup discussions at this time. He apparently had advised Bill Ramsay, a noted England administrator, against a cup but if it were introduced, the sport must retain control of it.

The next, and among the most influential, move came in a manner unexpected. There had been an attempt to introduce a professional rugby circus in 1977 with an entertainer, Lew Pryme, as its public face. The idea came to nothing and it seemed richly ironic that Pryme later became the executive director of the Auckland Rugby Union and was responsible, at short notice, for organising the opening ceremony for the first cup. In 1983, an Australian entrepreneur, David Lord, set about organising his own professional rugby troupe and while it too was ultimately unsuccessful, New Zealand and Australian rugby officials could see how big the writing was getting on the wall, even if their British colleagues still had to squint to see it.

Within six months of Lord's proposal being beaten off (and, essentially, it was defeated by a promise of money that was not delivered) the IRB tentatively and with considerable misgivings voted in March of 1984 in

Entertainer Lew Pryme who, in his rugby phase, went dramatically from poacher to gamekeeper.

favour of an Anzac feasibility study. Its resolution, with reluctance plain between the lines, read:

The Board remained divided on the basic concept of such a competition but accepted the New Zealand intention to prepare a feasibility study. It was finally agreed between Australia and New Zealand that both Unions would co-operate in the preparation of a feasibility study to be presented to the Board for consideration at its 1985 annual meeting.

The New Zealanders and Australians went off and hatched their plans. They set up an equal representation committee of eight and agreed that when it met in Australia, Nick Shehadie was chairman and when in New Zealand, Dick Littlejohn. They knew well the historic opposition of the IRB, especially that of Scotland and Ireland, but they cunningly sugared their pill when they eventually presented it in 1985 by arguing that a World Cup would be the saviour of amateurism.

The two countries began their presentation by saying their proposal was different to anything previously suggested because this time, rugby administrators would retain sole control: 'In this way, the "spirit of rugby" with all its amateur ideals will be preserved in a manner that will pre-empt any future threats of professionalism brought about by entrepreneurs outside of rugby's current framework.'

It further emphasised the point later in the document: 'It is essential Rugby administrations recognise a changing external environment, anticipate the needs of the sport and make changes within the overall scope of Rugby to meet these needs without in any way changing the ideals or principles of the sport. World Cup Rugby would make this possible.'

When the board met in Paris in March of 1985, the Anzac proposal for an inaugural World Cup in both countries in 1987 was agreed. Voting figures were not made public but it seems generally accepted that there was a healthy majority in favour. Scotland and Ireland voted against it and there was a suggestion by Wyatt in his book that the votes of England and Wales (two each) might have been split. The crucial votes were from the two South African delegates, Danie Craven and Fritz Eloff, who voted in favour even though they knew that neither the New Zealand nor Australian governments would allow South Africans into their countries to play.

Rugby thus took its first significant step onto the world stage. New Zealand and Australia were faced with the gigantic task of organising the first tournament in the space of about 18 months; but the whole rugby world, as it existed then, was faced with the paradox of trying to keep the game amateur while exposing it to the welcoming arms of professionalism. The year 1987 was chosen deliberately. If 1986 had been chosen, it would have left too little time for organisation and would have clashed with the Commonwealth Games, which essentially involved the same countries; similarly, 1988 was rejected because it would have locked rugby into the Olympic cycle and made marketing with all its attendant modern trappings more difficult.

The promise by the rugby administrators to keep the game amateur was one thing; the reality was quite another, as the astute officials in New Zealand and Australia charged with organising the cup surely knew.

As an Australian academic historian, Brett Hutchins of the University of Queensland, noted, the onset of the cup created considerable ideological tensions:

> On the one hand, the IRB's adherence to amateur practice ensured players could not be paid (at least openly) for competing in the 1987 World Cup,

thereby supposedly providing a 'powerful medium to demonstrate the strength of this [amateur] conviction' in the face of professionalism and commercialism in wider sporting practice. On the other hand, the IRB voluntarily accepted money from commercial entities such as television networks, corporate sponsors and advertisers who contributed to making the 1987 World Cup a moderate financial success.

There were tensions on the ground during the World Cup too. When the Irish team arrived in Auckland, its manager was Syd Millar, the former Ireland and Lions prop. Neither he nor the Irish union were yet fully convinced of the desirability of a World Cup, he said. The same Syd Millar 20 years later was chairman of the IRB and an enthusiastic supporter of the cup.

The difference between old English and modern New Zealand attitudes over what amateurism actually meant also led to some heat during the tournament. The English schoolteacher John Kendall-Carpenter, who headed the IRB committee overseeing the cup, was a little miffed when he saw various All Blacks from the World Cup squad appearing in television commercials. One in particular was of the whole squad in a commercial for the New Zealand union's new beer sponsor, Steinlager, and another was Andy Dalton, the injured All Black captain, endorsing Yamaha four-wheel farm bikes (or 'quads'). Kendall-Carpenter made known his feelings to British journalists and he promised he would have it all out with the New Zealand chairman, Russ Thomas.

The pair met in Christchurch to sort out the differences and after the meeting they fronted a press conference which became a shouting match with New Zealanders on one side of the commercial fence and British on the other. Kendall-Carpenter and Thomas were almost reduced to the roles of bystanders as journalists argued their interpretations to each other, the New Zealand view being that the regulations allowed the commercials and the British view — put most articulately by John Taylor, the former Welsh and Lions flanker turned television commentator — that the commercials

Ron Palenski Collection

Russ Thomas, chairman of Rugby World Cup Ltd at the time, with the Queen at the 1991 final.

were nothing less than full professionalism. There was a sense that Taylor and others were not so much arguing in support of amateurism *per se*, but arguing against anything that might give the New Zealanders an advantage over British players.

Both groups were right. In the haste to organise the cup, someone overlooked that the IRB regulations on amateurism were not exactly matched by the regulations governing the tournament. The IRB rules allowed players to appear in television commercials in certain circumstances so long as their involvement in rugby was not mentioned. Dalton, for example, in his commercial was 'Andy Dalton, farmer', or words to that effect. It was a disingenuous, but wholly legitimate, way around the rule.

The World Cup participation agreement, a wordy document which players had probably never seen, never mind read, was much more unforgiving. 'No member of the team,' it intoned, '. . . shall during the tournament directly or indirectly . . . allow his name to be used for advertising, give any public testimonial, or engage in any television or radio broadcast or cinematograph film or other recording . . .'

The whole fuss, played out in a room at the Christchurch headquarters of the company that Thomas managed, was a small but amusing (there's nothing higher than an outraged British journalist on a high horse) example of the tensions already swirling around rugby going global.

While the New Zealand and Australian initiators of the cup might have talked grandly about preserving amateurism (and thereby gaining political support), it was evident that the amateur days were rapidly drawing to a close. As Hutchins noted in his academic paper, 'The initiation and ongoing staging of the Rugby Union World Cup represents a formal reconfiguring of rugby's economic and cultural politics.' It transformed world rugby from international amateur sporting competition to professionalised global sporting commodity.

The form and content of rugby's administrative and cultural politics have shifted from sporting values and practices that once supported, sustained and reinforced amateurism to those that have established a new ascendant hegemonic order in the structuring and practice of rugby through which professionalism and commercialism have come to dominate.

Stripped of its academic speak, that means the game's no longer the thing. Money's the thing.

Cold Shoulder for Coach Jimmy

All Black coaches, as any one of them will acknowledge in private moments if not in public, are polarising figures. For every supporter who thinks one coach is the best the All Blacks have had, there is another who thinks him the worst. Most of the people airing their opinions on coaches have, it is almost unnecessary to say, never coached anything in their lives and if they have selected teams, they have done so in the luxurious comfort of knowing their teams will never take the field.

Whether it is from members of the public airing their opinions for free or members of the news media being paid to air their opinions, coaches are always a favourite target. Players, by and large, keep their opinions to themselves because they know that publicly denigrating a coach will not do their chances of future selection a power of good.

Whatever Graham Henry, John Mitchell, John Hart or any of their predecessors may think of a coach being the Aunt Sally for anyone who cares enough to tap a keyboard or punch in numbers on a phone, they can find solace in the knowledge that it has been like that since the dawn of coaches. In fact, what they have been through is mild compared with what the first All Black coach, Jimmy Duncan, faced.

None of them prompted a letter from players urging the New Zealand union to get rid of him. (At least not that the public knows about.) Duncan did.

None of them occasioned a special meeting of the union at which several provincial unions pushed for him to be dismissed. Duncan did.

There have been tales over the years, never documented and seldom proven, of players on tours deciding the coach wasn't up to it and taking over themselves. But only to a limited extent because the coach still held the whip hand through being able to select teams and had the authority of the New Zealand union behind him. The clever players who assumed the coaching role for themselves always made sure that the coach's dignity remained intact.

Not so for Duncan.

Duncan's history has been well documented before. How he was one of the dominant players in the late Victorian era and regarded as having a shrewd tactical brain, that he was a prime mover in adopting the distinctive New Zealand five-eighths pattern — and he was not above trying a trick or two to gain an edge over the opposition. He captained New Zealand in the first official test, in 1903 against Australia, and he was coach — the All Blacks' first coach — when the first test was played in New Zealand in 1904, against Great Britain in Wellington.

During the summer of 1904–05 the New Zealand union put together its plans for the first tour of Britain by a fully representative New Zealand team. It was a tour that for years had been longed for by New Zealanders anxious to test their rugby skills against the home of the game, colonials wanting to show the 'Mother Country' how well they had taken to the game.

Tours then were not organised in the way they later came to be. New Zealand had to pay to get the team to and from Britain and also pay all internal costs. The only way they could recoup some of their outgoings was through a percentage of gate money. The cost was one reason a British tour, first mooted in the mid-1890s, had not happened before. (For later tours, the host union paid all costs and took all receipts.)

The New Zealand union hit upon a debenture scheme to raise money. It asked all provincial unions to contribute but such was the poor response from the provinces, the national union had to dispatch the All Blacks to New South Wales for a quick trip.

The annual meeting of the New Zealand union in April of 1905 had approved the appointment of Duncan as coach for Britain without dissent. The problems with the appointment surfaced when the team was in New South Wales and the captain there, Jimmy Hunter, told the manager, Neil Galbraith, that a lot of players were unhappy about Duncan. The essential point seemed to be not so much about Duncan's personality — he could, by all accounts, be an irascible chap — or his ability but the belief that his presence on the tour would deprive a place for another player.

The coach the All Blacks didn't want, Jimmy Duncan.

Galbraith reported all this in a letter to Wellington and, in the meantime, provincial unions led by Auckland called for a special meeting of the New Zealand union to get rid of Duncan.

The argument turned nasty. The view in Wellington was that if the provincial unions got their way, it would be interpreted as a vote of no-confidence not just in Duncan but in the New Zealand union as a whole. That would then put the tour in jeopardy.

The union's chairman, George Dixon, found himself in a difficult position. Not only was he chairman, he was also the designated manager for the tour and was also the Auckland delegate to the national union. To avoid the embarrassment of conflict, the Auckland union sent its secretary, Charles MacCormack, to the special meeting.

Dixon hot-footed it to a Wellington legal firm, Bell Gully Bell and Myers, and sought the opinion of one of the most senior lawyers in the country, Francis Henry Dillon Bell, president of the Law Society, crown solicitor, former mayor of Wellington and a man of general all-round influence and standing.

Bell helped draft a public statement for Dixon which set forth the

New Zealand union's position. It made it very plain that if the provincial unions had taken up debentures in sufficient numbers as they were asked, any number of players could be despatched to Britain and the presence of Duncan would not be an issue.

It pointed out that no objections had been raised when Duncan coached the team in Wellington the previous year:

How much more important will it be to have a coach in the Old Country where thirty matches are to be played? The committee feel that it is of paramount importance to have someone available to closely observe the tactics of our opponents . . . and to advise as to the introduction of frequent and effective changes in the style of play to be adopted by our own men.

And then came the stinger in the tail:

. . . the committee would point out that they have appointed Mr Duncan as coach; that the liability they would be subject to were they to cancel the appointment is such that they cannot accept; and that, therefore, in the event of affiliated unions deciding that a coach shall not be sent, the committee have no option but to take this decision as a vote of want of confidence, and to leave the responsibility of cancelling the appointment of those who desire to accept it.

The special general meeting was held on July 18, a fortnight before the team's departure, and MacCormack duly moved the motion that the appointment of Duncan be cancelled because it was a grave error. He gained support from the Taranaki delegate, who seconded the motion, and 13 others, but nowhere near enough. Delegates in favour of retaining Duncan totalled 34.

For all the New Zealand union protestations that they could not afford another player, the Auckland forward, Bill Cunningham, was added in the week before departure and that, it seems, was sufficient to mollify Duncan's opponents for the time being.

The Wellington weekly newspaper, the *New Zealand Free Lance*, remarked in the week after the team had left for Britain:

> A pleasing feature about the departure of the team was that it appeared to be a body of men that practically understood one another. The 'bobbery' about the coach had died a natural death and most of the players agreed with a remark of George Smith's — 'When old Jimmy gives us the best of what he has got stowed away in his old bald head, he will be all right.'

It may aid understanding of that comment to know that Dixon was manager of the *Free Lance*.

In the unpublished diary that Dixon kept throughout the tour, he wrote soon after the ship had cleared Wellington Harbour: 'Duncan appears quite happy with rest of team and gives impression of being shrewd and a leader — decent fellow — don't anticipate any trouble in this direction.'

Dixon added later in the voyage: '"Uncle Jimmy" Duncan is making himself very useful and appears to be well liked by everybody.'

According to Dixon's diary, Duncan was at meetings on tactics with Gallaher, Stead and other players.

The truth about what happened on the tour will probably never be known. The captain, Dave Gallaher, and Cunningham apparently took charge of the coaching of the forwards and the vice-captain, Billy Stead, of the backs. In their 322-page book after the tour, Gallaher and Stead never once mentioned Duncan. Stead ignored him too in his voluminous correspondence to his local paper, the *Southland Times*.

That paper reported about a third of the way through the tour that relations within the team were strained. It was based on letters from players and said:

The trouble has apparently arisen out of the old sore feeling over the appointment of Jimmy Duncan as coach. The letters indicate that from the first the Auckland members set themselves up in sharp opposition to Duncan and then to the Otago members in general. A number of others, including Stead, had sided with the Auckland contingent and the general result has been that every attempt by Duncan to assert authority has been met with open hostility at meetings of the team while, on the field, he has been simply ignored.

One of the letter-writers was quoted as saying: 'He is just nobody.'

A contrasting view was offered by one of the star players of the tour, Billy Wallace, 26 years later. In his memoirs, he wrote:

Another man [after Dixon] who put in a lot of hard work behind the scenes was Jimmy Duncan. Not only had he been a clever player, but he was able to impart his knowledge to others . . . his coaching, especially in the early part of the tour, when we were working out our plans of campaign, [was] of very great value to us and helped to weld us into a powerful attacking combination.

Whether appreciated by the New Zealanders or not, at least one British newspaper writer had a high opinion of Duncan and much of his opinion had to have been shaped not so much by what he saw, but by what he was told by members of the touring party.

He wrote:

Out in New Zealand, they believe that Mr Duncan can win matches just by looking on. He is the brainiest footballer that ever donned a jersey. A football match to him is like a problem in chess. He stands in the enclosure and studies every move of the opposing side. Then he shifts a pawn, makes an opening for one of the second row pieces, and the result is usually a try.

This unidentified writer even likened Duncan to Napoleon and the All Blacks to Napoleon's marshals.

'The members of the team have rightly been described as modest,' he said. 'But I fear they lay aside their modesty when they begin to talk about Mr Duncan. Napoleon's marshals may have spoken of Napoleon in such terms, for they were very loyal men.'

The press also turned to Duncan at the end of the tour for comments on British rugby, perhaps because the public comments by Dixon and Gallaher were so brief and uninformative they might have been the origin of news media spin doctoring.

In the London *Evening Standard*, Duncan held forth copiously on what British rugby was doing right and what it was doing wrong. His general theme was that there was little, if anything, the New Zealanders learnt about rugby from their hosts.

> In either back or forward play, I have seen nothing throughout the tour by which we could improve the standard of rugby in New Zealand — not even in Wales. Our one defeat came about, not that we met a superior team, but because the majority of our backs were obviously out of form.

Duncan's praise of the All Blacks was not unstinting. 'Our present team has several faults which would be quickly condemned in New Zealand,' he said. 'They were not in my opinion the strongest combination we could put together, particularly in the forwards' ranks. I know of no less than twelve men in the Colony at the present time who would be an acquisition to our forces.'

Part of Duncan's brief was to assist the manager, which he did, and to play if necessary, even though he was retired. The only time he got on the field was in New York when he played for the All Blacks in an exhibition match against a team of expatriate Britons that was supplemented by some of the All Blacks.

PMs Plump for Pinetree

New Zealand's most celebrated rugby player, Colin Meads, had the support of both the present and a future prime minister of New Zealand after he was sent off against Scotland in 1967.

The prime minister at the time was Keith (later Sir Keith) Holyoake, who sent a message to the All Black management: 'It has become a weekly event to congratulate you all on another international victory, but I do so warmly on the occasion of your great victory over Scotland. We are most sorry about Colin Meads.'

The future prime minister was Geoffrey (now Sir Geoffrey) Palmer, who as a 25-year-old law student was engaged in research at Cambridge in England after gaining his doctorate at the University of Chicago.

Palmer and his wife Margaret had avidly followed the All Blacks in Britain and saw the Wales and England tests. Incensed by the sending off of Meads at Murrayfield, Palmer wrote a letter to the editor of *The Times*.

'There are a number of things about New Zealand rugby that followers of the game in the British Isles do not understand,' Palmer wrote.

Rugby is one of the central ingredients of New Zealand culture. The physical contact element has always been important in New Zealand rugby. There has been a tendency over here to regard this type of play as ungentlemanly and rough. New Zealanders, for their part, regard the style of rugby here as soft and effete.

Palmer then defended Meads:

> We had been taught at an early age that to ruck men off the ball was an essential part of forward play. Regarding the incident for which he was sent off, the television rerun made it clear enough that Meads was kicking at the ball which Chisholm was trying to gather. Whatever Chisholm's proximity, that would be regarded in New Zealand as quite unexceptional play.

Palmer said Britons may not like the way New Zealanders approach rugby, but should pause before condemning the way Meads behaved:

> He was playing in the way which makes him, to New Zealanders, the greatest forward ever . . . Judge him if you like. But remember, your standards are not catholic. There is more in heaven and earth than dreamed of in the British rugby philosophy. Ask the South Africans.

This unexpected defence of the All Blacks, one no doubt gratefully read by them, did not find favour with a prominent England rugby personality, Bernard Gadney, a Suffolk schoolmaster and former England halfback (he played against the All Blacks in 1936). He wrote a letter that was published three days later and said it would be a tragedy if players in the British Isles adopted a rough play policy with inevitable disregard for the spirit of the game and its laws.

Interestingly, he did not say in the letter, and neither did *The Times* add a comment, that he was a younger brother of the former referee, Cyril Gadney, who was one of England's two delegates on the International Rugby Board and, crucially in this case, was one of those who sat in judgment on Meads three days before he wrote the letter.

It became apparent that Meads, by being banned for two games, was sacrificed for the greater good of the game.

Meads, who was then approaching his 100th match for New Zealand, was sent from the field by Irish referee Kevin Kelleher just minutes from the end of the All Blacks' 14–3 victory against Scotland at Murrayfield.

Kelleher had earlier warned Meads for what he considered to be dangerous play when he trampled on a Scottish body on the wrong side of a ruck — something New Zealanders saw as just part of the game.

Having warned Meads, Kelleher was then bound by the game's laws as they were then to send him off if he caught him infringing again. About three minutes from time, the Scottish first five-eighths, David Chisholm, was in the process of gathering a loose ball when Meads lunged at it with his right foot. Kelleher deemed Meads's action to be dangerous and sent him from the field — becoming only the second player (after All Black Cyril Brownlie against England in 1925) to be sent off in a test.

Sympathy for Meads was widespread, especially and, naturally enough, in New Zealand.

In these days when yellow cards are common and red cards not infrequent, it is understandable if the impact of the Meads incident is underestimated. Only two players had been sent off in tests at that time and both were New Zealanders. It was an enormous story and dulled somewhat the impact the brilliant 1967 team had in Britain. Newspapers in Britain and New Zealand ran the story for days and in a discussion on BBC television, the former Welsh first five-eighths, Cliff Morgan, got into trouble with his countrymen for coming out in support of Meads.

The image of Meads trudging off Murrayfield on a grey, dull afternoon remains with New Zealanders still: the hands on hips, the head slightly bowed, a white head-bandage protruding from under a scrum cap. (The scrum cap, incidentally, returned to the Meads Te Kuiti farm with him but Meads's wife Verna did not like seeing it and being reminded of her husband's sending off, so gave it to a young Waitete player.)

NZ Rugby Museum

Referee Kevin Kelleher tells Colin Meads his game is over.

The sending off was not the end of it of course. On the following Tuesday, with the All Blacks by then in Cardiff, what was then known as an adjudicating committee met to decide whether the sending off was punishment enough for Meads, or whether some further penalty was required. It has been well recorded that he was suspended for two matches.

What has not been well recorded, if at all, is the way the justice was dispensed. The committee met in room 228 of the Angel Hotel in Cardiff — a fateful hotel for All Blacks — for nearly two hours and emerged with a simple statement announcing the suspension.

The committee comprised Cyril Gadney of England, Glyn Morgan of Wales and the New Zealand manager, Charlie Saxton. The International Rugby Board secretary, Eddie Kirwan of Ireland, sat in on the hearing and handed out the statement to waiting reporters. It said the committee supported Kelleher's action and contained the final sentence: 'Meads has been severely admonished and warned as to his future conduct and is suspended for the next two games on the tour.'

What it did not say, what it could not say, was that Saxton was not happy. Saxton was well respected in international rugby. He had been an All Black in 1938 and after rigorous war service, including a time with the risk-taking Long Range Desert Group, he captained the 2nd New Zealand Expeditionary Force team that did so much to resurrect international rugby after the war. Saxton was seen as central to the Kiwis' — as they were known — open, entertaining play and it was no coincidence that the 1967 All Blacks, managed by Saxton and coached by another of the Kiwis, Fred Allen, were seen, and still are by those old enough to remember, as one of the most pleasing All Black teams to take the field.

Saxton's public comments at the time about Meads were brief. He and Allen had watched replays of the incident and he felt that Meads had been treated harshly. But he made no criticism of the adjudicating committee or its decision — not publicly anyway.

It was a different story that he reported to the New Zealand union. Writing his fourth tour report from Cardiff on December 7, two days after the hearing, he said the hearing was particularly hard for him 'as I said I would accept the referee's statement along with the others. I had to anyway, but I fought hard for no further penalty or suspension'.

Saxton then made the telling comment:

Unfortunately, I was on my own and eventually had to compromise for a penalty of a suspension for the next two games. The consensus . . . was that Colin was very unlucky but the referee had to be backed up for the future of rugby football. The IRB, if you remember, gave strict instructions about this at their last meeting.

Unlike judicial hearings in rugby now, no lawyers were present and Meads did not appear before the committee.

Meads's non-appearance became the subject of a short, sharp exchange at the annual meeting of the IRB in Edinburgh four months later. Kirwan, the secretary, told the meeting of the Cardiff hearing. The minutes record: 'The Hon Secretary further reported that at the outset of the proceedings of the adjudicating committee, Mr Saxton was asked if he wished Mr Meads to be given an opportunity of attending before the committee and that Mr Saxton had replied in the negative.'

Ces Blazey and a former All Black, Jack Griffiths, were the two New Zealand delegates to the meeting. Blazey took exception to Kirwan's account of what happened and as a result, this sentence was inserted: 'Mr Blazey said Mr Saxton denied that he had declined an opportunity for Mr Meads to be heard.'

As a result of the Meads incident, the IRB reviewed its disciplinary procedures. Blazey and Griffith forced through a change that provided for a majority rather than a unanimous decision (which if in force at the time would have allowed Saxton to be a dissenting voice).

A more telling change allowed for the player ordered off to present his side of the story. The new regulation forced through by Blazey and Griffiths read: 'That the committee should have full discretion as to its procedure and as to what evidence it may require provided that the player ordered off shall have the right to be heard if he so desires.'

Rugby and War

A century ago it used to be a common view that rugby and what were called athletic sports generally were ideal preparations for war. Sport provided physical fitness and mental toughness, courage, endurance, initiative, self-reliance, loyalty and obedience, all qualities which could be transferred from the sports field to the battlefield.

The ideal soldiers, it was held, were those who were proficient in sport. This view grew up in Britain with the gradual development of organised sport in the 18th century and transferred to New Zealand along with other imperial baggage. The rise of rugby to be New Zealand's national sport coupled with reports of the prowess of New Zealand troops in the Boer War that spanned the turn of the 19th century led to what some historians have called the mythology of the New Zealand male.

'The connection between sport and war was widely appreciated,' eminent historian Keith Sinclair wrote. 'Rugby could be seen either as a preparation for war or as a substitute.'

Another historian, Jock Phillips, held that the 'male mythology expressed in rugby and war is not a peripheral aspect of New Zealand history, but central to a whole range of experiences'.

This view was not propagated just by historians looking back over their shoulders and trying to figure out why rugby became so important to New Zealand and helped shape the distinctive New Zealand identity.

One of the most noted early rugby personalities, Tom Ellison, the man who decided the New Zealand uniform would be all black and who captained the first New Zealand team, wrote of the 'good, manly and soldier-making game of rugby football'.

The premise was acknowledged too by newspaper editorial writers, especially one in the *Dominion* in September of 1915 when the campaign on Gallipoli was drawing to its failed end. It was commenting on the formation of a 'sportsmen's battalion' in Sydney and said: 'Field sports have played a very material part in the evolution of our national character.' (In this, the *Dominion* writer was not quite correct. 'Field sports' was a phrase used then to describe such pursuits as hunting, fishing and equestrian events, as distinct from 'athletic sports'.)

'From the point of view of physical fitness the athletic sportsmen are the elite of the community,' the editorialist continued, 'and they should be the first to place their services at the disposal of the state in times of national peril.'

The impression created by both contemporary and later reports was that sports people, and rugby players in particular, purposely pursued their sport as a prelude to war and that the former prepared them all the better for the latter.

There was special pride in rugby circles, Phillips said, when two prominent players became the only New Zealanders in the Boer War to be awarded the Victoria Cross and the Queen's Scarf for gallantry. A reasonable question to then pose would be: why should there not have been? There would have been equal pride, surely, in any circles to which garlanded soldiers belonged.

Central to the sport-training-for-war view is an assumption that teenagers and young men who played rugby did so in the likelihood that it was but a step along the path to war; that they were not playing for any reasons that are perfectly acceptable today — such as enjoyment, companionship, because they were good at it, or even money — but in the expectation they would one day exchange football for gun. The supposition that sports people may have been more fitted for war was an outcome perhaps, but not necessarily an intention.

Another obvious point is that rugby players, and men from other sports, prominent or not, signed up to go off and fight wars because they were of the age that was required; age and health were the determining factors imposed by military authorities, not whether a recruit was a rugby player. And given that rugby had such a hold on New Zealand, of course many of them were rugby players.

Of the just under 20,000 New Zealand deaths in the First World War, 13 of them were All Blacks, plus an unknown and unknowable number of provincial rugby players who were also killed, not to mention any number from other sports. The vast majority therefore were ordinary New Zealanders, just New Zealanders who signed up, did their duty and never came home again. Rugby was incidental among such numbers, which is hardly convincing proof that the sport was used as preparation for war or, if it was, what a miserable failure it turned out to be.

The 13 All Blacks, though, have not been forgotten. One of them was the captain of the All Blacks of 1905–06, Dave Gallaher, and since 2000 the All Blacks and France have played for a trophy named in his honour. The first All Blacks to go to Europe after the war, the 1924–25 team led by Cliff Porter, made a special trip from Paris to visit Gallaher's grave in Belgium. Other New Zealand teams have since followed suit. In 2004, with the All Black jersey now bearing an embroidered red poppy in remembrance of Gallaher and other All Blacks who died in both world wars, hooker Anton Oliver was asked to speak to the team about the significance.

To modern All Blacks, soldiers who died in a war as distant as the years between 1914 and 1918 are men from an ancient and unimaginable history. Oliver had to relate them to the current players. He spoke about the ages of those who died — roughly the same as the players to whom he was speaking. And to ram the point home, Oliver told 13 of the players in the room to stand — one for each All Black who had died. The point was not lost on the modern players.

If rugby was not seen by its players as preparation for war, there have nevertheless been acknowledgements of how rugby experience has served New Zealand soldiers well.

NZ Rugby Museum

The Originals' captain, David Gallaher, as a corporal in the Mounted Rifles in the Boer War. Gallaher served in the Sixth and Tenth New Zealand contingents and returned as a regimental sergeant-major.

Perhaps the point was made best by John Mulgan, a writer who was not known for his rugby prowess and who would not have fitted into any mould of a New Zealand rugby stereotype (unless the average rugby follower counted the early English epic poem 'Beowulf' among his favourites). Mulgan wrote about seeing New Zealanders again in the Second World War after living in Britain for some years.

> Most New Zealanders can look back on some game which they played to win and whose issues then seemed to them then a good deal more important than a lot that has happened since. This phenomenon is greatly deprecated by a lot of thinkers who feel that an exaggerated attention to games gives the young a wrong sense of values. This may well be true, and if it is true, the majority of New Zealanders have a wrong sense of values for the whole of their lives. But to be frank . . . I found in wartime that there was a considerable virtue in men who had played games like professionals to win and not, like public schoolboys and amateurs, for exercise.

Rather than see similarities between New Zealander and Englishman, Mulgan saw differences. New Zealanders, he wrote, found it easier to get down to the moral plane of a German soldier while the Englishmen spent some time and casualties in finding war ungentlemanly before they adapted.

> I don't know that the cunning and professionalism of my fellow countrymen is to be commended on abstract grounds, but these are comfortable qualities to have about in wartime. Oddly enough I don't think these things affected their natural kindliness nor the kind of ethics that they expect from people in private life. It was only that they looked on war as a game and a game to New Zealanders is something that they play to win, against the other side and the referee, if necessary.

134

Mulgan's view was a compelling one and had been expressed before by other writers, New Zealand and British, though perhaps not as eloquently. When New Zealand played their first test in Sydney in 1903, there were several published remarks about how the players from 'the other side' brought an intensity to the game not previously seen in Sydney. One example was that it was common for New South Wales players at the time to stop whenever an infringement had occurred rather than to wait for the referee's whistle. The All Blacks, however, played to the whistle and in fact scored one try through the Australians stopping when a New Zealander stepped into touch but the referee did not pick it up.

There were several similar comments about the different approach the All Blacks brought to the game when they were in Britain in 1905–06. Such comments continue to echo down the years.

While New Zealand imported rugby from the English ruling class that established it, not all of the game's trappings were adopted. Strict amateurism was one of them and Ellison once argued that the concept of players not being given expenses when away from work on tour was never meant to apply anywhere beyond southern England. The New Zealand union only reluctantly became guardians of the amateur tenet.

The attitude that playing rugby was but preparation for war, or even for the greater game of life, was an English one that did not travel comfortably.

The companionship of rugby, rather than its supposed martial tendencies, was illustrated in a story told by Jim Burrows, an All Black in 1928 and an officer of field rank during the Second World War. Burrows told how Fred Hanson, the chief engineer of the 2nd New Zealand Division, went to see a company of his sappers working on a section of the front beneath the grim, German-held heights of Cassino. The section was held by Free French troops and as Hanson approached where the New Zealand engineers were, he saw a rugby match was in progress under the shelter of some high ground. There were no posts. The touchlines were marked only by New Zealand and French soldiers in uniform. The players themselves were also in uniform.

As Hanson drew near, Burrows related, he wondered why he had not seen kicking of any sort. It soon became clear: there was no ball — in its place was a dead fowl.

Burrows continued by quoting a Frenchman who spoke to Hanson:

'What is it about sport,' he asked, 'that it can bring people together in this way? Here at Cassino, under conditions that, to put it mildly, could only be described as dangerous, two armies from foreign countries, neither speaking the other's language, suddenly decide to play a game of football. They have no jerseys or studded boots, no marked field and no football posts. Indeed, they have no football. But does that bother them? Never. They take the field as if they were at Twickenham. Tell me, what is the appeal, what is the magic of this game called rugby, that under such conditions, grown men will play it with a dead fowl?'

This surely was why people played rugby — because of its 'magic', its appeal.

Rugby was a central part of the welfare programmes organised by the military for troops during both world wars. Unit and battalion matches were common, sometimes against other New Zealand teams and sometimes against British, Australian or South African teams. The New Zealand army organised teams in both France and England after the armistice in 1918 and the best of the players were chosen for the team that won an inter-Allied tournament and subsequently toured South Africa.

The commander of the 2nd New Zealand Expeditionary Force in the Second World War, Bernard Freyberg, personally ensured that rugby was an essential part of his soldiers' recreation. From the first, in 1940, he told Brigadier Tom King, Director of Ordnance Services and a former member of the New Zealand Rugby Union council, to get rugby started; Burrows, King and a former All Black captain, Jack Griffiths, were designated the selectors for the first NZEF team to play an 'international'. Towards the end of the war, Freyberg — who had played senior club rugby in Wellington as a youth and was once sent off for punching — again took the initiative in planning for a 2NZEF team to tour Britain once the war ended. This team became the Kiwis, captained by another former All Black, Charlie Saxton.

Freyberg was not a distant general. He kept a close eye on things rugby as well as things military. King related how he submitted, as was his habit, a team to play United Services. Named at centre was Ray Mahony, who had played for both Otago and Southland. Freyberg went through the team carefully and, according to King, the following conversation ensued:

Freyberg: About this Mahony, is he as good as [Jack] Sullivan? [Sullivan was one of the starring All Blacks against South Africa in 1937 and was later All Black coach and chairman of the New Zealand union].
King: Oh, I wouldn't like to say that sir, but he is very fit and a very good footballer.
Freyberg: Then why haven't you picked Sullivan?
King: Sullivan is near Tobruk, sir.
Freyberg: That doesn't matter, I'll fly him back.
King: Oh, I don't think that will be necessary sir. Mahony is fit and I don't suppose Sullivan is. Anyway, I'm quite happy with Mahony.
Freyberg: Well, this will be a very strong team you're playing. I've offered you Sullivan and you won't take him. Mind they don't beat you.

Fortunately for King, his team won.

Sullivan, whose wounds in the fighting in Libya ended his playing career, often remarked in later years that the services games were not recreational, social affairs. They were a serious business, especially matches against South Africa, and Sullivan and another All Black soldier turned administrator, Tom Morrison, both argued the standard of teams was at least the equal of the best of New Zealand provincial sides.

Rugby has been often touted as the most egalitarian of games, at least in

Bernard Freyberg, 'The General', but by then the Governor-General, is introduced to the 2NZEF Kiwis in Wellington by captain Charlie Saxton.

New Zealand, but this was put to the test in army matches because officers played alongside non-commissioned officers and privates. Paul Donoghue, a Wellingtonian who was a regular member of the 22 Battalion team, recorded once playing with a Major (later Brigadier) Tom Campbell.

The officer was running strongly down the touchline but Donoghue could see that he was covered. Donoghue was unmarked on his inside and shouted, 'With you Major, pass to me sir!' The major kept running. Donoghue repeated: 'Inside sir, inside!' Still nothing. Donoghue then bellowed: 'Pass you selfish bastard, pass!' The major did and Donoghue scored. Nothing was later said about the use of offensive language towards an officer.

This may have been indicative of the equality of rugby, about which a one-time chief justice (and rugby player), Sir Richard Wild, said that there is 'no yielding to status in a tackle, there's no privilege in a scrum'.

Or it may also have been indicative of the easy relationship, based on

138

mutual respect, between officers and ordinary soldiers in what they called 'the Div'. There's a story, perhaps only slightly embellished, of when Freyberg and General Sir Bernard Montgomery's successor as commander of the Eighth Army, General Sir Oliver Leese, were having a cup of tea on the balcony of a villa in Naples after discussing the future deployment of the New Zealanders.

An ocean-going yacht appeared from around a point and gently sailed within hailing distance of the two generals. A group of soldiers was on board, laughing uproariously and clearly not, like their superior officers, drinking tea.

'G'day Tiny,' one shouted raucously. 'How are ya mate?'

Another joined in: 'Tiny! Ya bloody beaut!'

Leese looked coldly at Freyberg: 'Who on earth are they, Freyberg?'

Freyberg: 'Oh, they are probably my chaps.'

Leese: 'Where did they acquire the craft from?'

Freyberg: 'Oh that. They probably pinched it.'

Freyberg's interest in the welfare of the soldiers under his command was demonstrably genuine. The 2NZEF Kiwis, whose name among services teams has lived longest, was Freyberg's idea not at the end of the war but soon after the start. Wellington and Petone rugby stalwart Mike Whatman chronicled the extraordinary venture that was the Kiwis and based most of what he wrote on the recollections of the players and of their manager, Captain (later Brigadier) Allan Andrews — 'the Brig'.

Freyberg was at dinner with his headquarters staff in Cairo in 1940 and predicted the war would be a long one but at the end 'I want a team of soldiers representing the New Zealand Division to undertake a rugby tour of the United Kingdom.' He said, 'It will help put the game back on the map and at the same time be of value in providing a nucleus of experienced players to assist post-war rugby in New Zealand.'

Freyberg was true to his word. No sooner had the war ended than Andrews issued orders calling for nominations for the team. Three former All Blacks, Vic Butler, Jack Hore and Ron Stewart, were appointed selectors.

Nominations flowed in from along the trail that New Zealanders had traversed over six years of war from Cairo to Trieste. Several of the triallists had come from prisoner of war camps and one of those who was eventually chosen, Pat Rhind of Canterbury, had been a guest of the Germans since the debacle in Greece four years before.

Some of them had had 'hard' wars and perhaps none more than the Kiwis' captain, Charlie Saxton. He was initially seconded to a secret unit in Australia, a group intended to operate behind Japanese lines in Southeast Asia, then transferred to Egypt where he was assigned to the Long Range Desert Group, whose specialty was raiding German airfields and supply depots far beyond the front line. At one point, Saxton's unit was sent by the British to the Greek Dodecanese islands until Freyberg and the New Zealand Government realised where they were and protested. The Prime Minister, Peter Fraser, wrote that New Zealanders were 'stupidly sacrificed' and that a British explanation for their presence there was rejected contemptuously.

Freyberg had suggested to the New Zealand Government — rather than the New Zealand Rugby Football Union — that it cover all costs for the tour and Prime Minister Fraser readily agreed. Freyberg laid down four aims: to help revive interest in rugby in Britain; to aid services charities; to benefit New Zealand rugby; to play bright, open football.

The tour succeeded on all fronts. It had both a contemporary impact and left a lasting legacy. Sixteen of the players became All Blacks. The only previous All Black in the team was its captain, Charlie Saxton, and he became manager of the 1967 All Blacks who were coached by another Kiwi, Fred Allen, who remains the most successful coach the All Blacks have had. That 1967 team, captained by Brian Lochore, was regarded as the most exciting side in Britain since the Kiwis.

The legacy of the war, or more specifically military service, was noticeable in New Zealand rugby for years afterwards. Leading administrators such as Tom Morrison, Jack Sullivan, Charlie Saxton, Ces Blazey and Jack Griffiths (the last-named an aide to Freyberg) all bore the hallmarks of their army background. It may not be fashionable to note now, politically incorrect even, but they and others of similar background had a demeanour and bearing different from those who had not served. There was, too, a mutual understanding and respect that only shared danger and privation can engender. Even Terry McLean, the rugby writer who had served in the Middle East and in the occupation force in Japan, carried his army days with him for the rest of his life: it was in the carriage of his step, it was in the way he spoke and it was most obvious when a senior officer was in view. He was once at a reception at New Zealand House in London more than 30 years after the war and a senior British officer, resplendent in beribboned dress uniform, hove into view. McLean, cynic that he could be, visibly stiffened and all but saluted.

The army, like rugby, could never leave such men. Rather than playing rugby as preparation for war, their wars both spared them and prepared them for the rest of their lives.

Among the New Zealanders who went to France and Belgium in 2007 for the 90th anniversary commemorations of the Battle of the Somme were two old soldiers from the Second World War, two mates who served together and played together: both members of the 2NZEF Kiwis, both All Blacks, Bob Scott and Fred Allen.

Lieutenant F. R. Allen, 27th Battalion, was 87 years old. Driver R. W. H. Scott, Army Service Corps Tank Transport, was 86.

They stood facing the Menin Gate, the emotively symbolic archway that straddles the main road out of Ypres, through which hundreds of thousands of soldiers marched to their deaths between 1914 and 1918.

They stood ramrod straight as they once had on the parade ground; their stomachs in and their chins up, their thumbs rigid down the seams of their trousers, just as the sergeant-majors used to bark at them to do.

The years fell away as they marched in step towards the gate, there to pay their homage. The army and rugby were with them still.

The Versatile Mr Smith

When the two New Zealand teams which toured the United Kingdom and Ireland between the world wars were in northern England, in 1924–25 and in 1935–36, they were met by a middle-aged man with a pronounced limp and a Lancashire accent. He was, according to Gordon McLean, journalist and provincial rugby player (and brother of All Black Hugh and of writer Terry), a remote and detached figure. He showed an almost pathetic eagerness to pick up the threads of his earlier life, McLean wrote.

He may not have been recognised by the All Blacks, and the limp and the accent surely would have given no clue about his background, but once they knew his name any doubt was erased. The stranger in their midst was one of their own; in fact, one of the greatest athletes New Zealand has had and surely the most versatile.

He was named William George Smith when he was born in Auckland in September of 1874, but to New Zealanders and followers of rugby, league and athletics in Australia and Britain, he was George Smith: champion hurdler and sprinter, try-scoring All Black wing, pioneering league player and, most surprising and most disputed of all, a champion jockey.

There is no disputing the bullet points of his achievements: between 1898 and 1904, he won 15 New Zealand athletics titles (four of them at the one championship meeting in Wellington in 1900), five Australasian titles (New Zealand and Australia combined for a championship meeting until 1928), and one English Amateur Athletic Association title.

He was chosen for every All Black team for which he made himself available, most memorably the 1905–06 tour of Britain and Ireland. He scored 19 tries in the 19 matches in which he played and by far the most crucial of them was his try that gave New Zealand the lead late in their first test against Scotland. 'The scorer . . . was embraced and literally wept over by his fellows,' commented the Edinburgh *Evening Dispatch*, 'and if they did not kiss him, well, they came very near to it. Their delight was natural for it meant that they had won their first international.'

Smith had a collarbone broken in the 23rd game of the tour, against Munster, and had to miss the England and Wales tests. Smith's absence from the Cardiff match, when Wales won 3–0 and Bob Deans had the disputed 'try', has been lamented ever since, an absence that was as damaging to the All Blacks' chances as that of their vice-captain and strategic architect, Billy Stead. Had Smith played, McLean wrote, 'it is highly improbable that New Zealand would have lost the match'.

Smith played just one more match on tour, against Glamorgan County, and back in New Zealand in 1906 he played just four more times for Auckland, giving him an improbable record of just 11 matches for Auckland over a 10-year period. He had made his debut in 1896 (in the same match as future captain Dave Gallaher made his first appearance for Auckland) and played for New Zealand for the first time the following year.

After touring Australia with the All Blacks, he helped Auckland inflict on Wellington its first defeat on its home ground for 20 years. This was the first game for Wellington for 18-year-old Billy Wallace. Wellington led 4–3 with only 10 minutes to go — and then Smith scored two great individual tries, running from over halfway on each occasion. 'It was George Smith who won the match for the northern province, for he scored a couple of beautiful tries,' Wallace recalled. 'The winning try was a masterpiece. He received the ball in the loose near the touchline between the twenty-five and halfway, and ran right through the Wellington backs and round the late Johnny Baumber, who was playing fullback, to score.'

Smith's rugby career thereafter came second to athletics. He played only sporadically, not appearing for either Auckland or New Zealand again until 1901, and then not again until 1905. It was clear Smith only took to rugby seriously again when a tour was in the offing.

His absence from the rugby season in 1902 can be easily explained because that was when he and a Christchurch miler, Bill Simpson, went to Britain to compete in a series of meetings, including the English AAA championship meeting, where Smith won the 120 yards hurdles. They were sent by the Auckland and Christchurch athletics centres, the costs of their return passages being raised by public subscription. There had been a move two years earlier to send Smith to the Olympic Games in Paris, but through a lack or organisation or a lack of money, or both, nothing happened. Smith would have been the first New Zealander to compete at an Olympics had he gone to compete for Australasia (New Zealand and Australia combined to send teams to the 1908 and 1912 Olympics).

Smith was compared with the best in the world when he competed in England in 1902. The English AAA championship meeting was regarded at the time as a surrogate world championship in the days before the formation in 1913 of the International Amateur Athletic Federation, and when the Olympics were still in their formative stages. It was not until 1983 that the first official world athletics championships were held.

The winner of the 120 yards hurdles at the two previous English championship meetings was American Alvin Kraenzlein, described by his coach, Mike Murphy, of Penn State University, as the world's best all-round athlete of his time. He won four gold medals at the 1900 Olympics in Paris and pioneered the modern practice of hurdling with the leading leg extended. Other hurdlers, Smith included, used the contemporary 'side-saddle' style. The hurdles themselves were nothing like the lightweight models of today. They were shaped like farm gates — made of timber and 3 feet 6 inches high and 6 feet wide. New Zealand athletics statistician Peter Heidenstrom once drily commented that the hurdles were ideal because if an athlete hit one, they were just the right size to serve as a stretcher as well.

In Kraenzlein's absence in 1902, Smith was expected to win and he did, cheered on by the chant of 'Smithy' from a group of New Zealand soldiers who were in Britain on their way home from the Boer War. He gained little credit from English athletics writers, however. 'A quaint, old-fashioned figure is Smith,' the Manchester *Evening News* reporter commented. 'Not in the least cut out for hurdles, Smith looks what he is — a sheep farmer.' That was a large slice of journalistic licence. The closest Smith ever got to being a sheep farmer, or any other sort of farmer, was when working as a butcher for Hellaby's in Auckland.

The *Illustrated Sporting and Dramatic News* said Smith was not in the same

Ron Palenski Collection

Mr Versatile — George Smith.

class as Kraenzlein and hinted heavily that Smith's record must have benefited from favourable timekeeping in New Zealand. The English papers also said Smith had been slow to start the championship final and only took the lead with one hurdle left. This was disputed at the time by 'Prodigal' writing in the Sydney *Referee*, who said it was well known that Smith was one of the fastest starters in the sport. 'Prodigal' knew what he was talking about because that was the pseudonym for Richard Coombes, one of the leading sports administrators and athletics judges on both sides of the Tasman and later a member of the International Olympic Committee.

A month after the race, when Smith was back in New Zealand, 'Prodigal' wrote: 'I hear that Smith's version of the 120 yards hurdles championship does not tally with the English press reports. He says, I am informed, he was quicker away and stayed in front throughout the race.'

The English *Athletics News* writer was convinced that Smith was not as good a hurdler as the man who was second, Alfred Trafford of Birmingham, who had also been beaten by Kraenzlein the year before. 'I am convinced that had Trafford's health and business allowed him to have proper training, he would have beaten the winner who is, to say the least, a disappointing hurdler. Style he lacks and he has not too much pace.' Smith gave the lie to that when he met Trafford in a handicap race. He gave him two yards and beat him by two yards.

The English writers' view of Smith's achievements may well have been coloured by their dislike of colonials taking English titles. Americans and Irish were regular winners at the English championships but a winner from 'Maoriland' may have been an incursion too far.

Whatever the view of the English writers, Smith's record and ability at athletics was undoubted, just as it was in rugby.

Not so his achievements as a jockey, though. Smith, at the age of 20 and weighing 7 stone 9 pounds (48.5 kg) rode a horse called Impulse to win the New Zealand Cup at Riccarton in 1894. There's no doubt that Impulse won the cup that year and no doubt that a G. Smith was the jockey, but was he the same G. Smith who gained a later and wider fame in rugby, athletics and league?

One of the underlying causes for doubt was that while jockey Smith was a mere stripling in 1894, the rugby-playing Smith was said to be 11 stone 12 pounds (75.2 kg) when he was first chosen for New Zealand in 1897. Could he have added more than 20 kg to his weight in three years or, conversely, could he have shed weight to ride Impulse and still had enough strength and fitness for the demanding task of riding a horse in such a race?

The conundrum is encapsulated in the entry on Smith on the New Zealand Rugby Museum's website (www.rugbymuseum.co.nz):

> Smith was 20 years old in 1894 and it hardly seems logical that as a mature adult he could have ridden a winning mount at a weight of 7 stones 9 pounds, then just a few years later played top rugby weighing nearly four stones heavier. Had Smith wasted to reach his horse's handicap, then surely it would have sapped the strength needed to control a massive animal.

The crux of the doubters' argument therefore is weight and it rests on the statistic of Smith's weight given at the time of his first selection in the New Zealand team in 1897. It has to be accepted that the weight Impulse carried was rigorously controlled, but were controls so rigorous with the vital statistics of rugby players? Stories about false weights, heights and ages abound in rugby history. In Smith's case, he was listed as 11 stone 12 pounds in 1897 and that weight stuck to him, according to most sources, for the rest of his playing career. But why should that be so? Is that credible? In Smith's case, his age was wrongly recorded in the early days — he was said to have been born in 1872 and therefore 33 at the start of the 1905 tour. In fact, he was born in 1874 and 31 at the start if the 1905 tour. Scepticism of the weight ascribed to Smith in 1897 is further reinforced when it is noted that in his subsequent matches for New Zealand, in 1901 and on the 1905–06 tour, precisely the same weight was given.

When the All Blacks were in Liverpool in 1993, Smith's two daughters and grandson joined the players for breakfast. Among the All Blacks at breakfast was Jeff Wilson, who was on his first All Black tour after earlier that year playing cricket for New Zealand. After learning of Smith's achievements, Sean Fitzpatrick leaned across to Wilson and said, 'Hey Goldie, here's someone who's done more than you.'

The daughters and grandson were adamant that Smith was also the cup-winning jockey and said he'd told them about it and that they had newspaper clippings. All three have since died. Smith himself died in 1954.

A letter from one of Smith's daughters, Edna Stanfield, written in 1972 to Rod Chester, who was then compiling statistics on All Blacks for *Men*

In Black, which he and Neville McMillan first published six years later, has since come to light.

Stanfield leaves no room for doubt: 'The connection with horseracing started when he ran away from home in Auckland to become a jockey and rode many winners as a 6-stone lad and rode right through in steeplechasing to being 12 stone.'

Smith 'ran' to the Takanini stables run by his brother Fred, a noted trainer at the time and Stanfield noted that Smith was cured of childhood asthma because of the outdoor life and the constant smell of manure. It was also while with his brother at Takanini that Smith became interested in running.

Before Smith had a wider fame and enthusiastic if misguided claims might have been made for his versatility, the *Evening Post* in Wellington commented on the selection of the New Zealand team to tour Australia in 1897: 'G. Smith, the Auckland rep back in the New Zealand team, is reported to be a first-class horseman, having ridden Impulse in his first races and a successful hurdle jumper.' Similarly, after the Australasian athletics championships in Auckland in December of 1901, 'Prodigal' of the Sydney *Referee* described Smith as 'the crack Auckland athlete — footballer, pedestrian and horseman.'

Having been to Britain twice, first as an athlete in 1902 and then with the All Blacks in 1905, Smith went a third time in 1907. He was one of the first to sign up with the first New Zealand league team, organised by a Wellington postal clerk, Albert Baskerville. Known formally as the New Zealand professional football team and informally as the 'Professional All Blacks', they also came to be known as the 'All Golds', a pejorative play on All Blacks playing for money. Baskerville and Smith were acquainted through athletics and the pair compared notes on league after the All Blacks had returned from Britain. Smith was a prize signing for the new venture and clearly influential in persuading other leading rugby players to join.

At the end of the tour, Smith was one of five players who decided to stay in Britain. He signed with Oldham and his signing-on fee of £150 allowed him to send for his fiancé, Edith Kemble in Auckland, and the pair were married in Brighton on August 10, 1908. Smith played 173 games for Oldham until 1916 when, at the age of 40, he retired. What finally brought an end to his career was a badly broken leg rather than age. The break, sustained in a game against Rochdale Hornets, was poorly treated and the bones never knitted back together properly and Smith was left with a permanent disability.

As Gordon McLean noted: 'It is one of the ironies of his career that one of those straight and symmetrical limbs, which had carried him over the turf and over the hurdles like a gazelle, should have been, for the last 40 years of his life, bent and misshapen.'

Smith had intended to return to New Zealand. Plans were made and tickets bought for a return in 1920 until Edith Smith contracted food poisoning after eating kippers. She died within five days and the travel plans were cancelled.

Smith worked as a textile machinist but returned to Oldham at the club's request when he was 58 to be the first team's trainer. He did this for three years, then worked as a groundsman at a cricket club and during the Second World War — in which his son George was killed when a prisoner of the Japanese — he worked as a security officer for a haulage company. He retired at the age of 70 and, according to his daughter, 'loved to go racing with my husband in his later years. He loved his cigarettes and pint of beer and used often to say he trained on beer.'

1893 — The 'Berth' of the All Blacks

The first All Black team, the first to be organised by the recently formed New Zealand Rugby Football Union, should have, it has to be assumed, left with the cries of well-wishers ringing in the players' ears. It was the first team, after all, pitting the rugby skills of one colony against that of New South Wales, then known as the 'mother colony'.

It would have been expected that the players would have had the best of berths in the ship heading for Sydney, an 1893 equivalent of today's players flying business class with always a chance of getting bumped up to first.

But no. The players left bitterness and accusations and counter-accusations in their wake as they headed on their historic journey. Even their carrier, the Union Steam Ship Company, was accused of deliberately trying to sabotage the team's chances. At the root of the rancour was that New Zealand was not a united rugby colony. Canterbury, Otago and Southland had refused to join the NZRFU, which had been formed two months before the team's departure, for a variety of reasons, the main one of which seemed to be a fear that the union's formation would eat into provincial autonomy and centralise power in Wellington.

The reason, it appears, that the USS Company, then the biggest trans-Tasman shipping company and one of the most successful commercial operators in the Tasman world, became trapped in rugby politics was that it was Dunedin-based and therefore assumed to be sympathetic to Otago's parochialism.

There was no hint the night before the departure that anything was untoward. As was to become the norm for departing teams, there was a reception at Parliament and three of the politicians, each of whom had links with Auckland clubs, told the players of their responsibility as individual and collective representatives of New Zealand. It was expected, the players were told, they would bring nothing but credit on the country of their birth.

This last point was significant as the secretary of the New Zealand union, Ernest Hoben, made clear. He said it was not just a New Zealand team but a New Zealand native team because the manager and all the players (with one exception) were born in New Zealand. It was more native than the New Zealand Natives — a largely Maori side — who had toured Britain and Australia five years before. The warm glow at Parliament was replaced by a frosty atmosphere the next day when the players trooped up the gangplank of the *Wakatipu*, a ship designed to carry passengers, general cargo, coal and livestock on the trans-Tasman run. Expecting to be housed in the classier saloon berths, the players were instead directed into steerage and, in the words of the *Evening Post*, 'a most unpleasant contretemps marred the departure of the team'.

The *Post*, which was an avid supporter of the New Zealand union and employed Hoben as a parliamentary reporter, presented a subjective account of what happened. According to the newspaper, Hoben a month previously had booked 30 saloon berths for the team and three days before departure had given the shipping company the names of the men who would be occupying the berths. The paper said:

> Relying on the promises given, no further steps were taken until 5 o'clock yesterday [the day of departure] when a number of the men went down with their luggage in order to put it into their berths and found that 17 of them were expected to sleep in the steerage, above which several hundred sheep were penned, and that the Union SS Company had let to others the saloon berths which they had engaged to provide for the New Zealand team, and that further they were expected to share the steerage with a number of characters so questionable that they were advised by the captain to give him all their money and valuables.

One player supposedly recognised among the questionable characters a man who had, in his words, 'taken him down' for £10 on a racecourse.

The players, with manager George Campbell and Hoben, refused to bunk down where they were told and went to the company's office. According to the *Post*, the berths promised the players had been double booked and they were told they would have to sleep where they were put or not go at all.

> It was represented that in the case of at least one man who had already suffered severely from seasickness, the consequences of remaining in the sheep-tainted atmosphere would be absolutely dangerous and that in the case of all of them a voyage made under such conditions would so completely throw them out of form as to seriously affect their chances of success in their earlier matches.

Word evidently got around the crowd waiting on the wharf to farewell the team and there was shouted advice to the players as they made their way back to the ship to take possession of the saloon anyway. This the players did and a steward gave them blankets so they could sleep on the floor.

'It is absolutely certain,' the *Post* said, 'that the singular action of the Union Company will have a very serious effect on the success of the team and so unaccountable did it seem that the opinion was expressed by some that it had been done with this object — a thing which hardly seems conceivable'.

Among the farewell speeches a message of good wishes from the Governor, Lord Glasgow, was read and apparently one of the players responded: 'And after that, we are to sleep in a sheep yard.'

Hoben sent a cable to Sydney asking that the first game, against Parramatta district, be delayed a day to allow the players more time to overcome the effects of the trip.

The *Post* in an editorial called the Union Company's action 'very discreditable' and made the link with Otago and Canterbury not joining the New Zealand union.

Ron Palenski Collection

The *Wakatipu*, the ship on which the All Blacks had to share quarters with 'questionable characters'.

In fact, it would seem as though, because Dunedin and Christchurch were not represented in the team, the Union Company considered the representatives of the rest of the colony quite unworthy of any consideration — even that of keeping faith with them as to the arrangements previously made for their conveyance.

It also took the opportunity to make a general attack on the company, saying it needed to pay more attention to the Wellington–Sydney trade and that it should use more modern ships than the 'old fashioned, slow' *Wakatipu*.

The Wellington reporting of the team's departure did not go unnoticed in Dunedin. 'Football notes' were written in the *Otago Witness*, the weekly offshoot of the *Otago Daily Times*, by 'Forward', a pseudonym for James (later Sir James) Hutchison, who was later editor of the *Otago Daily Times* for 37 years and was at different times president and secretary of the Otago Rugby Football Union.

The accusation by the *Post* that the footballers were deemed unworthy of consideration because they came from neither Dunedin nor Christchurch was a ridiculous assertion, Hutchison wrote. 'After this, no one need feel surprised at the lengths to which the New Zealand union party will go.'

He showed little sympathy for the players. Relating how they did not have individual cabins, he commented:

> . . . it was only natural that persons like the members of the so-called representative team, accustomed to the most luxurious surroundings in their own homes, should turn up their haughty noses at the accommodation which for a matter of four or five nights they were to put up with on the *Wakatipu.*

Hutchison had no sympathy for Hoben, a fellow journalist who almost single-handedly brought together the New Zealand union. He said he was told by an authority in the Union Company that Hoben knew nearly three weeks before departure the nature of the players' accommodation on the ship. Hutchison said he was not surprised 'the patience and good temper of the staff was severely tried by the uncompromising attitude taken up by Mr Hoben'.

And he called contemptible the suggestion the company had any idea of interfering with the success of the team. 'But it must be remembered that the New Zealand union rests on a foundation which has been built up by reckless assertion and unworthy insinuation.'

As it happened, the New Zealanders beat Parramatta 8–0 in their first match, though the Sydney reporter noted a lack of practice and combination was evident and some of the players had not 'recovered their shore legs'. That's hardly surprising. They arrived in Sydney at 1 o'clock in the morning and played that afternoon.

Another 10 games were played, with only one loss, they received a 25–3 thumping by New South Wales in mid-tour. That loss was avenged in the final match when the All Blacks beat the state team 16–0.

The tour came seven years before federation and the separate colonies of New South Wales and Queensland chose not to field a joint Australian team.

Rotation Nothing New

One of the modern fashionable criticisms of the All Blacks or, more specifically, of the coach and of his employers, the New Zealand union, was that far too many players were being called on to wear international rugby's best-known jersey.

The professional era with its increased number of test matches and very rarely anything but a test, allied with a heightened awareness of sports science and player welfare, has meant that New Zealand's top side — however that may be determined — does not always take the field. The changes go by the name of 'rotation', a necessary policy for its supporters, a dirty word for its opponents.

Those who argue against rotation argue that the jersey is being devalued by the number of players who wear it in any given year. Those who argue in favour could well say that teams are still chosen to win test matches and if that ever changed and more tests were lost, only then the jersey could truly said to have been devalued.

But there's nothing new in any of this. Rotation, or to give it another more familiar name, 'selection', has been around as long as the All Blacks have been. If the black jersey is being devalued by the number of players being chosen to wear it, then it has always been devalued.

The much-maligned John Mitchell usually gets the blame for introducing the concept of 'second-string' teams when he took the All Blacks to Britain and France at the end of 2002 and left 21 of his best players behind — and promptly lost to England and drew with France.

NZ Rugby Museum

The 'third' All Blacks of 1949, the team that lost to Australia while the main side was in South Africa.

But he was far from being the first.

All Black history is riddled with teams that were not of the first choice and, in some cases, not even of the second choice.

There are well documented occasions, such as in 1949 when the All Blacks lost two tests on the one day — one in South Africa and one in Wellington — and some less well documented. Some were in the mists of a rugby time that no one now living saw but others were so recent that it is something of a mystery that modern rotation has any critics at all.

The All Blacks of 1905 are both the best known and least known in New Zealand rugby history. One famously toured Britain, France and North America, made the All Black name popular, lost to Wales and set many of the touring patterns which were to follow. The other was chosen after the Originals had left for Britain and played Australia in New Zealand for the first time. This team of players not deemed good enough for Britain beat the Wallabies 14–3 in Dunedin.

The fielding of one All Black team at home while another was away became something of a norm. When Australia toured in 1913, the All Blacks chosen to play them in the first test comprised players who had already been chosen for a tour of California. After the team left for the United States, a completely different All Black team played the second and third tests.

In 1921, when South Africa toured New Zealand for the first time, New South Wales also toured (Queensland rugby having gone into recess, New South Wales in effect became Australia for most of the 1920s). The All Black team to play the state team was originally intended to be made up of players who had not been involved in the three tests against South Africa, but in the event three of the test players were included.

Two months after the Invincible All Blacks' northern hemisphere tour of 1924–25, an entirely different New Zealand team — including 21 new All Blacks — set off for a tour of Australia. The New Zealand union decided the Invincibles had been away from home enough so figured a whole new squad was appropriate and would do the job — and it did, although it lost to Wellington before leaving then lost to a New South Wales Second XV when on tour.

Three years later, another batch of 18 new All Blacks was chosen to play New South Wales in New Zealand while the first-choice team was on its way home from the first tour of South Africa. The newcomers, though, were bolstered by the great midfield back, Bert Cooke, who had not been available for South Africa, and by the Invincibles' captain, Cliff Porter, who had not been chosen for the South African tour.

The next tour of South Africa, in 1949, was the occasion for one of the most bizarre years in New Zealand rugby. Not only did the team in South Africa lose all four tests, but the side chosen at home to play against Australia also lost both of its tests.

It's the only year in which the All Blacks have lost six tests, although by two different teams.

Multiple All Black teams were less frequent in the 1950s and 1960s but another unusual practice came into play in 1960 to add to the number of

All Blacks. When the New Zealand team was in Australia on its way to South Africa in 1960, two games were arranged in Sydney for the same day, a curtain-raiser against Queensland and the main event against New South Wales. The intention was so coach Jack Sullivan could give all his squad of 30 a game before arriving in South Africa but illness and injury thwarted that plan so local help was enlisted. A Sydney club player, Maurie Graham, and an Australian wing, Eddie Stapleton, both became All Blacks for the day — and because they took the field as All Blacks, All Blacks they remain.

Something similar occurred in 1970 when New Zealand were again on their way to South Africa. Two games were arranged in Perth, again to give the whole squad a run, but Sunday play meant that the All Black halfback, Sid Going, was unavailable. Chosen in his place was a young Perth medical student, Jamie Hendry, who, again, forever remains an All Black.

The following tour of South Africa was another occasion for new All Blacks, but in a different context. In 1976, New Zealand rugby broke new ground by sending a team to Argentina for the first time. One stipulation for its selection was that none of the players who had already been to South Africa would be considered so it was in effect a third New Zealand team that went. Only four previous All Blacks were included — John Callesen, Andy Haden, Peter Sloane and Ian Stevens. They, like all the other additional teams, were regarded by the New Zealand union as full New Zealand representatives. This was made specific by the New Zealand chairman, Ces Blazey, who was asked if the players in Argentina would be regarded as All Blacks. He replied that 'All Blacks' was purely an unofficial term but that they were full New Zealand representatives.

Some of the players questioned their status while they were in Argentina and their coach, Jack Gleeson, made an impassioned speech at a team meeting telling them what the black jersey and the silver fern meant and that his charges were fully fledged members of rugby's most exclusive club.

By the end of 1976, 56 All Blacks had taken the field.

Argentina provided the next example of the wider selection policy.

The Pumas toured New Zealand for the first time in 1979 and played two matches against New Zealand, though neither was recognised as an official test (because such rarified heights then were reserved solely for member countries of the International Rugby Board). France had played two tests in New Zealand earlier in 1979 and the All Black teams chosen to play the Pumas excluded anyone who had played against the French.

There was a similar occurrence in 1980 when New Zealand played Fiji in Auckland. It was intended that the All Black team comprise players who had not toured Australia earlier that year but in the event it did include two who had toured.

Adding validity to the rotation policy in recent years has been the almost total disappearance of tour matches. On old-style tours, All Black teams played twice a week, Tuesdays or Wednesdays and Saturdays, and, in theory at least, all players at the start of a tour were deemed to have a chance of test selection. So teams were mixed around to find the right combinations and so players could get a chance to impress the coach ahead of test selection. It was not unusual for a player to play in a midweek match and then play again in a test on the following Saturday; or to play in a test on a Saturday and front up again on the following Tuesday. The longer a tour went on, the whole squad became settled into a midweek team and a test team. Now, coaches are denied the chance of seeing their charges playing in a New Zealand combination against provincial or club teams so experimenting at test level is the only option.

Modern rugby's — and television's — insatiable demand for test matches has had a dramatic effect on player statistics. Just to use two examples: the man generally regarded as the best of All Blacks, Colin Meads, played 133 times for New Zealand in his career that went from 1957 until 1971, but 'only' 55 of those matches were tests and that was a record until broken by Gary Whetton in 1989.

By contrast, the most recent All Black captain, Richie McCaw, at the start of 2008 had played in 59 matches for New Zealand — and every one of them was a test.

Needlecraft:
The Fred Allen Way

Toward the end of 1998, New Zealanders took a more than usual interest in the progress of the South African rugby team. The Springboks beat the All Blacks on both occasions they played in 1998, but that wasn't the sole reason for the heightened interest in their progress.

New Zealand beat South Africa 55–35 at Eden Park in 1997 and the Springboks had not lost a test since. As they embarked on a northern hemisphere tour late in 1998, they had won 14 tests in a row. That meant they were heading for the record 17 tests in a row won by the All Blacks between 1965 and 1969.

Test win No. 15 came when South Africa beat Wales 28–20 at Wembley, helped along by a penalty try. New Zealand interest was in more than just whether South Africa would maintain their unbeaten record. It was the first match for Wales' new coach, Graham Henry, and the competitiveness of the Welsh — especially after they had been beaten 96–13 in Pretoria earlier in the year — earned him the nickname 'the great redeemer'.

South Africa's next opponents also had a New Zealand connection. The Leslie brothers, Martin and John, sons of 1974–76 All Black captain Andy, were 'kilted Kiwis' in the Scottish side beaten 35–10 that gave the Springboks their 16th win.

Ireland were coached by another New Zealander, Warren Gatland, and they became victim No. 17 for South Africa. The record was shared.

The last test of the tour, against England, gave the Springboks the chance of removing the All Blacks from the record books. England is not normally the team of choice for New Zealand rugby followers, but the team led by Lawrence Dallaglio must have had more Down Under support than it ever has.

'The Needle' — Fred Allen.

Pieter Rossouw scored the first try but thereafter England, relying on a dominant pack, took control and won 13–7. South Africa were denied sole ownership of the record and the Springbok coach, Nick Mallett, said he thought the 17 wins in a row might never be bettered.

A South African journalist, Dan Retief, found it was apt that New Zealand and South Africa would share the record. It seemed historically appropriate that two such great rivals should be deadlocked, he wrote.

It might also be seen as fitting that the All Blacks' great run began against South Africa — and was ended by South Africa.

The 1960s have taken on the warm glow of nostalgia. That decade might be remembered in Britain as the swinging 60s or in the United States as a decade of protest and psychedelic free love: Colin Meads does not slip easily into either of those images. Meads in gaily-coloured flowing robes, roman sandals, long hair and moustache does not come readily to mind.

The nostalgic reproduction of New Zealand in the 60s has Meads as the indomitable face of All Black rugby, the sheep-toting farmer down from the King Country hills bent on wreaking destruction among any rugby team that dared challenge the might of New Zealand.

It was the era when farmers seemed to dominate the All Black jersey, even if that was more urban myth than rural reality. There were farmers, of course. Stan Meads played alongside his brother in five of the 17 tests; Brian Lochore was a constant through the era, so too other farmers Ken Gray, Sam Strahan, Ian Kirkpatrick and Sid Going, and others such as Kel Tremain with close farming connections.

It was an era of quiet, comfortable competence, an era in which New Zealand rugby was guided for the most part unerringly by Fred Allen, a man known as 'The Needle' for the sharpness of his tongue and no one dared mock that in his day job he was a manufacturer of dresses. ('The Needle' moniker appears to have been bestowed on Allen by the Taranaki and All Black five-eighths, Neil Wolfe. The Auckland team that Allen coached was training in New Plymouth on a Sunday morning after playing Taranaki on the Saturday and some of the Taranaki players, including Wolfe, watched Allen make his players sweat out their after-match indulgences. 'I used to give them a bit of stick,' was Allen's dry comment.)

Allen was coach of the All Blacks for 14 of the 17 tests. They unfolded like this:

Test No. 1, v South Africa, Auckland

This was the fourth test of the 1965 series and South Africa went into it with a chance of squaring the series. Against predictions, they had won the third test in Christchurch and had played well since. But the All Blacks had other ideas. Their pack was unchanged throughout the series and the fourth test in Auckland was the farewell to their popular captain in a record 30 tests, Wilson Whineray. Such milestones are not marked by losses. The first half was as tight as any encounter between the two teams touted as the best in the world. The only score was a try by flanker Dick Conway, the man who five years earlier had had a finger amputated so he could tour South Africa. The second half was all New Zealand's. Tiny Naude, the lock whose kicking won the Springboks the third test, kicked a penalty goal early on but that was all they got. North Otago's first All Black, Ian 'Spooky' Smith, scored twice and tries were also scored by Bill Birtwistle and Ken Gray. Fergie

All Blacks pay tribute to their captain, Wilson Whineray, after his final test.

McCormick, playing in his first test, kicked a conversion and the first five-eighths, Mac Herewini, kicked a dropped goal.
New Zealand 20, South Africa 3

Test No. 2, v British Isles, Dunedin
The Lions team captained by the Scottish soldier, Mike Campbell-Lamerton, continues to be burdened with the tag of being the worst Lions team to tour New Zealand (though that may have been challenged in 2005). There were some fine Lions players, but they happened to come up against an utterly dominant New Zealand team coached for the first time by Allen. Three tries to none told the story.
New Zealand 20, British Isles 3

Test No, 3, v British Isles, Wellington

This was the Lions' best test performance. Their captain, Campbell-Lamerton, had to make way for the Welsh lock, Delme Thomas, and the pack was also strengthened by the addition of the redoubtable Irishman, Willie-John McBride. The Athletic Park surface was vintage 1960s mud, but it was still an entertaining test with both sides trying to play attacking rugby. The All Blacks again scored three tries to none.
New Zealand 16, British Isles 12

Test No. 4, v British Isles, Christchurch

The All Blacks fielded an unchanged side for the third test in a row for the first time in 63 years of playing tests. Thomas this time played in the front row for the Lions, allowing Campbell-Lamerton to regain his place. The score was 6–6 at halftime but the All Blacks came away in the second half for a conclusive win. This time it was three tries to two.
New Zealand 19, British Isles 6

Test No. 5, v British Isles, Auckland

Allen made the first change of the series when Malcolm Dick replaced Ian Smith on the right wing. Campbell-Lamerton continued his game of musical chairs and was again left out, the captaincy reverting to first five-eighths David Watkins, who had led them in the second test. The All Blacks were true to their pattern, wearing the opposition down in the forwards and setting the backs free. Three of the All Blacks' four tries were scored by backs. This was the first time the Lions lost all four tests on tour.
New Zealand 24, British Isles 11

Test No. 6, v Australia, Wellington

This was the only home test of 1967 and was played to mark the 75th anniversary of the founding of the New Zealand Rugby Football Union. It was a gala occasion in Wellington with a smorgasbord of reunions and other

functions coinciding with the test and culminating in the official anniversary dinner. It was the first test for Sid Going and the last for Waka Nathan. The All Blacks scored four tries, two of them by a former national sprint champion, Tony Steel.
New Zealand 29, Australia 9

Test No. 7, v England, London
The All Blacks went to Britain in 1967 after a proposed tour of South Africa was cancelled. It became one of the great All Black tours, Allen and the manager, Charlie Saxton, with captain Brian Lochore a willing ally, inculcating into the players the free spirits of the 1945–46 army team that Saxton had captained. The All Blacks had their biggest win against England with the match marking something of a rugby resurrection for the first five-eighths, Earle Kirton.
New Zealand 23, England 11

Ron Palenski Collection

Fred Allen tells three of his kingpins, Brian Lochore, Kel Tremain and Colin Meads, what he wants.

Test No. 8, v Wales, Cardiff

This was still the era when Wales were seen as the toughest opposition and the ultimate of tests. It was the first time Gareth Edwards and Barry John teamed up in the scarlet of Wales against New Zealand. For all their youthful brilliance, the game was won and lost in the forwards. The decisive move came in the 13th minute of the second half when Bill Davis pounced on a loose ball near the Welsh posts. Wales missed several penalty goal attempts in their vain attempts to close the gap, one of them by Edwards.
New Zealand 13, Wales 6

Test No. 9, v France, Paris

This may have been the finest performance by the All Blacks on their 1967 tour. At least the man from *The Times*, Uel Titley, thought so. It was magnificent rugby, he said, and raised the game to an art. It started off as a fairly violent game and Titley made the comment: '. . . the influence of Lochore's restraint and dignity as captain was particularly felt'. Allen made significant changes to his first-choice team. He picked Sid Going ahead of Chris Laidlaw and Ian Kirkpatrick, for his first test, ahead of Kel Tremain. France led for a time in the second half but the All Blacks, again through the power of their pack, re-established their authority and added tries by Kirkpatrick and Malcolm Dick. A try to Steel in the first half, his sixth in six tests, was worth the trip to Paris alone, Titley wrote.
New Zealand 21, France 15

Test No. 10, v Scotland, Edinburgh

This is the match remembered more for the sending off of Colin Meads than for the result. By the time Meads was dispatched by referee Kevin Kelleher, the scoring had all been completed. Scotland led first after a dropped goal by Meads's 'victim', David Chisholm, but Fergie McCormick evened the scores soon after with a penalty goal that gave him 100 points for the tour. Ian MacRae scored the All Blacks' first try against Scotland since 1935 and his Hawke's Bay partner, Bill Davis, added another in the second half. It has seldom been remarked upon that this test was Lochore's first at lock — he moved there after Meads had been sent off.

New Zealand 14, Scotland 3

Test No. 11, v Australia, Sydney

Name the All Black who went on as a replacement and scored three tries. This test provides the answer. Brian Lochore had a broken thumb and a hamstring injury and Ian Kirkpatrick went on for him, the first replacement since the International Rugby Board had finally relented to allowing them. Kirkpatrick was on the field for 58 minutes, during which he scored three tries. Earle Kirton, Tony Steel and Chris Laidlaw also scored. This was also the match in which Australian halfback Ken Catchpole was so badly injured he was forced to retire. Colin Meads was roundly criticised in Australia then and later for being the cause of Catchpole's injury, trying to drag him from a ruck when he was trapped.

New Zealand 27, Australia 11

Test No. 12, v Australia, Brisbane

This match so nearly brought the streak to an end. The Wallabies led 12–11 at halftime after a try by halfback John Hipwell and three penalty goals by fullback Arthur McGill. McGill kicked another early in the second half but the All Blacks responded with a try by Grahame Thorne. McGill kicked another goal and Australia led by four. With two minutes to go, Bill Davis attacked and kicked ahead. Following up, he was tackled by centre Barry Honan and hometown referee Kevin Crowe gave the All Blacks a penalty try. Fergie McCormick's conversion from in front preserved the All Blacks' record.

New Zealand 19, Australia 18

Test No. 13, v France, Christchurch

This was another close-run thing. The match was all kicks until the last seconds when the score was tied at 9–9. Fergie McCormick had kicked three

penalty goals and Pierre Villepreux two, one of them out of the mud from 45 metres. With a draw probable, France messed up a defensive scrum and the ball slid along the ground to Villepreux, who fly-kicked for touch. It rebounded off Thorne back into in-goal, however, and Earle Kirton seized the moment and the ball and scored the winning try.
New Zealand 12, France 9

Test No. 14, v France, Wellington
It was one of those Athletic Park days when the weather dictated play. This time it was a strong northerly that swept down the ground. The only points of the first half were from a monstrous penalty goal by Pierre Villepreux, variously estimated at between 65 and 70 metres out. Fergie McCormick kicked three more orthodox penalty goals in the second half when the All Blacks had the benefit of the wind. It was a more aggressive test than most and referee John Pring lectured both captains at one point.
New Zealand 9, France 3

Test No. 15, v France, Auckland
This marked the end of Fred Allen as All Black coach, completing an era whose hallmark had been attacking 15-man rugby that won praise in New Zealand and, even more hard-won, in Britain. Fittingly, Allen's final match was a fine example of the type of rugby he demanded and the French obliged as well. France outscored the All Blacks three tries to two, but superior kicking by Fergie McCormick made the difference.
New Zealand 19, France 12

Test No. 16, v Wales, Christchurch
Wales came to New Zealand as Five Nations and triple crown winners and with a growing reputation. Much was expected of some of the Welsh players, especially the inside back pair of Gareth Edwards and Barry John and the young fullback, J. P. R. Williams. But they had only one warm-up match,

against Taranaki, and their off-season form was nowhere near good enough for a rampant All Black team. The All Blacks scored four tries to none and equalled their best winning margin against Wales. The Welsh hooker, Jeff Young, had his jaw broken by a punch, which gave Colin Meads fodder for his patter in his after-rugby career as a celebrity speaker.

New Zealand 19, Wales 0

Test No. 17, v Wales, Auckland

If this was how the streak would end, though no one knew it at the time, it could not have ended in a better way. The All Blacks' win was a rugby eruption, according to Terry McLean. Appropriately, given that it was just over a month before Neil Armstrong set foot on the moon, the eruption 'blasted Wales's rugby reputation into outer space,' McLean wrote in *The Times*. The All Black fullback, Fergie McCormick, would have been over the moon. His personal haul of 24 points from three conversions, five penalty goals and a dropped goal was a world individual record (beating the 22 points set by Daniel Lambert of England in 1911). It was the last test for one of the stalwarts of the winning run, Ken Gray.

New Zealand 33, Wales 12

In those days when tests were infrequent highlights of the rugby year, the All Blacks did not play again until they toured South Africa in the following year and on Saturday, July 27, 1970 — just over 13 months after the Welsh test — New Zealand were beaten in a test for the first time since 1965. The Springboks won the first test 17–6, New Zealand came back to win the second 9–8, but the Springboks won again 14–3 and then 20–17.

The coach of the All Blacks then was Ivan Vodanovich, the former prop who had also been coach against Wales. One of the frequent but unanswered questions of New Zealand rugby was why Fred Allen did not extend his winning run so he could have a tilt at the biggest rugby windmill of them all, South Africa. Everything was in Allen's favour. He had earned a reputation as the leading coach in world rugby — especially at a time when some countries still thought a coach was the vehicle that took the team to the ground — and the All Blacks by 1970 were still substantially those he had picked, nurtured and coached.

South Africa was the ultimate prize for any All Black, coach or player. New Zealand had never won a series there (and did not until 1996). It was a tantalising magnet for anyone involved in New Zealand rugby. Its pull should have been even greater for Allen, given that he was captain of the team that lost the series there 4–0 in 1949. To go back and gain revenge would have been the triumphal summit of his career.

Instead, he quit. He never said why at the time and thereafter refused to elaborate or to answer any of the many speculative theories which have done the rounds over the years.

There is a strong suspicion that it was rugby politics which were the root cause of why Allen did not have the chance he should have had. In a country that has many times demonstrated its delight at cutting down poppies which have grown too tall, Allen was the tallest of the rugby poppies. Even more, he was an Aucklander. A successful Aucklander. Rugby then, as it had been for many years, was controlled rigidly from Wellington, by a small group of men holding positions of power and influence within the New Zealand union. It was precisely this Wellington grip on power that made unions such as Canterbury, Otago and Southland stay out of the New Zealand union when it was first formed. They feared what would happen but in the end, for the sake of their own rugby, they had to join.

Vodanovich was a Wellington man. He was of the inner circle. When he was made coach of the All Blacks in 1969, he was also on the New Zealand union's ruling council, a rare combination of appointee and appointer. His partner and patron in a Wellington menswear business was Tom Morrison, who was chairman of the ruling council from 1958 until 1969. Vodanovich was a likeable and much-liked enthusiast who worked hard and without

Ron Palenski Collection

Fred Allen lays down the law at training. His successor, Ivan Vodanovich, listens too.

monetary reward in the cause of rugby up to his death in 1995, but as a coach, he could never match Allen, let alone surpass him.

Rugby history, New Zealand history, could have been much different had Allen coached the All Blacks in South Africa in 1970. Had the All Blacks won that series, and they could have won it with Allen, the obsession about returning there in the quest for elusive victory would have been diminished. The anguish of the 1970s and 1980s may not have been as great.

		17-MATCH WINNING STREAK (1965-69)	New Zealand					Opposition				
			t	c	p	dg	total	t	c	p	dg	total
1	1965	South Africa	5	1		1	20			1		3
2	1966	Lions	3	1	2	1	20			1		3
3		Lions	3	2	1		16			3	1	12
4		Lions	3	2	2		19	2				6
5		Lions	4	3	1	1	24	2	1	1		11
6	1967	Australia	4	4	2	1	29	2		1		9
7		England	5	4			23	2	1	1		11
8		Wales	2	2	1		13			1	1	6
9		France	4	3	1		21	1		3	1	15
10		Scotland	2	1	2		14				1	3
11	1968	Australia	6	3	1		27	1	1	2		11
12		Australia	3	2	2		19	1		5		18
13		France	1		3		12			2	1	9
14		France			3		9			1		3
15		France	2	2	2	1	19	3			1	12
16	1969	Wales	4	2	1		19					0
17		Wales	3	3	5	1	33	2		2		12
Totals			54	35	29	6	337	16	3	24	6	144
Points per			x3	x2	x3	x3		x3	x2	x3	x3	
Total points			162	70	87	18	337	48	6	72	18	144

PLAYERS IN **17-MATCH WINNING STREAK (1965–69)**

17 Colin Meads

16 Bruce McLeod

15 Brian Lochore

13 Ken Gray, Ian MacRae, Kel Tremain

12 Chris Laidlaw, Fergie McCormick

11 Earle Kirton

10 Bill Davis, Sam Strahan

9 Tony Steel

8 Ian Kirkpatrick

7 Malcolm Dick, Brian Muller

6 Jack Hazlett, Alister Hopkinson, Mac Herewini, Grahame Thorne

5 Sid Going, Tom Lister, Stan Meads, Waka Nathan, Ron Rangi, Graham Williams, Mick Williment

4 Bill Birtwistle, Wayne Cottrell, Ian Smith

3 Michael O'Callaghan

2 Alan Smith

1 John Collins, Dick Conway, Tony Kreft, John Major, George Skudder, Owen Stephens, Wilson Whineray

First of the Bad Boys

The New Zealand Rugby Football Union — without the word 'football' since 2006 — gets itself offside with its constituent provinces from time to time and seldom does a year, or even a month, go by that it is not being criticised for some real or imagined deficiency.

Nothing is new in rugby.

However much aggrieved modern administrators may feel when fielding the slings and arrows of outraged provinces, or from an outraged public, they can take solace from the past. Invariably, there's been a more contentious issue, a more acute crisis.

The All Blacks toured Australia in 1897 and played and lost to Auckland on their return. The match was played on a Saturday afternoon but most of the players had to stay in Auckland until the Monday to catch their ship south. Players from both teams were given a post-match dinner at the Metropolitan Hotel on the Saturday night and things just carried on from there, as they can do sometimes.

The All Blacks' manager was a 35-year-old Wellington tailor, Isaac Hyams, who was also treasurer of the New Zealand union. He didn't like what he heard as the players filled in their time until their departure and he fingered three of them for 'disgraceful conduct' when the New Zealand union management committee met in Wellington on the following Wednesday night.

William 'Cocky' Roberts, a Wellington midfield back or wing who had joined the team as a replacement — and that was an issue in itself,

Joe Calnan, a Wellington loose forward, and William ('Pat') Harris, an Otago hooker, were all suspended immediately pending an inquiry. (Roberts joined the All Blacks in Australia as a replacement without the national selectors knowing or approving. When Jimmy Duncan was injured, Hyams cabled the Wellington union direct and told it to send Roberts.)

The charges, beyond the nebulous misconduct, were never made public but it was widely reported that drunkenness and bad language were involved, and there were also suggestions that Ellen, the wife of future All Black captain Dave Gallaher, had been the target of obscene language. Gallaher, then in his second season of representative rugby, had played for Auckland against the All Blacks.

Within a week, the national union decided the charges against Calnan and Roberts were proven but held off deciding about Harris until he had a chance to reply. This Harris eventually did, admitting the substance of the charges was correct but denying vehemently that Ellen Gallaher had been abused.

James Hutchison, a member of the Otago Rugby Football Union committee and a journalist who hid behind the pseudonym of 'Forward' when writing for the *Otago Witness*, judiciously noted that 'it would hardly be right that I should at this stage comment upon the fact that three members of the New Zealand team have been reported for misconduct at Auckland'. He then proceeded to do precisely what he thought it right that he not do: he commented.

The essence of his argument was that the incidents occurred when the tour was practically over and that the players should have been cut some slack. 'Indeed, if what I was told of the occurrence is true, the matter is one which need have given no occasion for a report to the New Zealand union had the manager of the team exercised that firmness at the outset which he should have managed,' Hutchison wrote.

What annoyed him most was that the Otago player, Harris, was treated differently from the other two. He contended that the Wellington union influenced the New Zealand union to act speedily in the hope that their two men would get off and thus be free to play in an upcoming game against Auckland.

> Their cases were actually disposed of and they were convicted before the copy of the complaint reached the Otago player. The practical effect of that is that the latter player's case is, to all intents and purposes, dealt with before he has been afforded an opportunity of defending himself. Anything more unfair and more un-English could hardly be conceived.

The New Zealand union had not in fact 'disposed' of the cases; it had found Calnan and Roberts guilty but deferred consideration of a penalty 'until further information has been received'.

Harris and the other two Otago players in the team, Jimmy Duncan and Barney Armit, had meanwhile been welcomed home as conquering heroes. 'They were welcomed on arrival by a very large crowd of footballers and others interested in the game, and were accorded an exceedingly hearty reception — being, in fact, almost mobbed by their friends,' the *Otago Witness* reported.

Nearly a month after Hyams first reported the three players, the New Zealand union management committee acted: it suspended each of the three for two years.

This news provoked another outburst from Hutchison who, if not speaking for the Otago union, must at least have had the unspoken support of it. He had a range of objections to the suspensions. He contended the provincial unions should have had jurisdiction over their players but he admitted he gave up on that because he had long since stopped trying to understand the NZRFU's by-laws.

He was also critical of the Wellington union not being given a copy of the evidence against Calnan and Roberts. 'The more one sees of the actions of the New Zealand union, the more must one be convinced of the utter perversity of those who are connected with it,' he wrote.

Hutchison's other argument against the suspensions was based on the fact the tour was over and that the incidents occurred in a public hotel. He wrote:

'Cocky' Roberts, Joe Calnan and 'Pat' Harris.

I have yet to learn that a player is responsible to a union for what occurs in his hotel, or his lodgings, or his private residence. He is under those circumstances amenable to the law of the land and if he misconducts himself there is a remedy, either civil or criminal, against him. The extreme limit of a union's power in these conditions would, I submit, be reached if it resolved that the offender should not again be chosen to represent it, but to say that he shall not play for his club seems to me to be grossly overstepping the mark.

Hutchison may have had a point if the tour was over, but the fact players were still in Auckland meant they were still under the jurisdiction of the New Zealand union.

He also argued that Hyams had not stayed in the same hotel as the players and had not personally seen or heard the misconduct and therefore had to rely on hearsay evidence.

As to what occurred on the Saturday and Sunday, I am credibly informed that gross exaggerations have become current concerning it and that had the manager displayed an atom of tact and judgment, the whole occurrence would have been prevented. However, he has apparently been desirous of showing what unpleasantness one clothed with a little authority, as he temporarily was, can create, and he has afforded the New Zealand union an opportunity of adding another blunder to its long succession of mistakes in the past.

The New Zealand union, curiously, asked the Wellington and Otago unions to endorse the punishment it had meted out.

The two Wellington clubs to which the players belonged, Melrose and Poneke, protested to the New Zealand union about the manner in which the hearings were conducted but they were told they should have directed their letters to the Wellington union, not New Zealand. The Wellington union eventually considered refusing to endorse the suspensions but the motion against was defeated on the casting vote of the chairman. The Otago union decided to take no action for or against endorsement until it saw the evidence.

The affair dragged on another month and then the New Zealand union wrote to Wellington and Otago saying it was 'a slip of the pen' that they were asked to endorse the penalties.

This 'melancholy confession of incompetence' was more grist to Hutchison's mill that ground away at the New Zealand union. It dreamt up the idea of the 'slip of the pen' so it could accept the Otago union's refusal to endorse the penalties. But even that idea did not come from the New Zealand union. It came from an outside source, Hutchison wrote,

for at the last meeting of the central committee in Wellington a letter was read from the Canterbury union inquiring why it was required to endorse the disqualification of a higher body than itself.

It is an indication of a certain dawning of intelligence upon the minds of the executive of the New Zealand union that they recognise that a slip of the pen, which is a mild expression for a blunder, has been committed by them.

The matter came up again at the national union's annual general meeting in April of the following year. Otago proposed a notice of motion that the suspensions be overturned and a delegation from Wellington argued the same. There was also a petition from 14 members of the 1897 team seeking pardons for their team-mates. For an unstated reason, it was not signed by any of the three Canterbury players.

The proposal that the suspensions be overturned was put to the annual meeting and it was defeated 27 votes to 7. It seemed to have gone unremarked that, judging by the content and tone of the various newspaper stories, and also of Harris's presence in Dunedin, neither the players nor their representatives ever appeared before any hearing. They were tried and sentenced *in absentia*.

All of this was played out against a constant stream of vituperation against the national union by Canterbury, which argued long and often that it should not be based in Wellington. (Canterbury and Otago, with Southland, it should be remembered, originally opposed the formation of a New Zealand union and stayed out of it for its first two years.)

Canterbury during 1897 had canvassed the other South Island unions about forming a South Island union, such was its dissatisfaction with the way business was handled in Wellington. The annual meeting also voted on Canterbury's move to have the national union based somewhere other than Wellington. This was lost 21–15. The only five unions in favour were Southland, Otago, South Canterbury, Canterbury and Marlborough.

None of the three suspended players donned an All Black jersey again.

Joe Calnan was considered a chance for the 1905–06 tour of Britain, but stopped playing after not being selected. He returned for just one game for Wellington in 1906.

Pat Harris did not play first-class rugby again.

'Cocky' Roberts played for Wellington until 1903.

Coates —
The Fight for Wright

Conservative Prime Minister Gordon Coates during the general election campaign in 1925 had emblazoned on his campaign posters: 'Hon. Gordon Coates — The man who gets things done'.

Not the previous year he wasn't.

Coates and his former boss, Prime Minister William Massey, were at the centre of a very public row on the eve of the departure of the All Blacks for Britain in July of 1924. This was the team that history now knows as the Invincibles for their unbeaten tour record, but there was little faith in them before they left.

The row involving the two most senior members of the Reform Party, the predecessor of the National Party, had nothing to do with their normal business, but all to do with the selection of the All Blacks. It was a rare incursion by the government into team selection, something that Coates later acknowledged was no part of his mandate.

The extraordinary situation arose because of dissatisfaction, especially in Auckland, with the All Blacks on a preliminary tour of Australia and in pre-departure matches against Auckland and Manawatu-Horowhenua, especially the Auckland match. They'd been beaten by New South Wales in their first match and then lost to Auckland on their return, just a few hours after disembarking from their ship.

The loss to Auckland prompted a stinging criticism of the team from one of the 1905–06 All Blacks, George Tyler. Writing in the *New Zealand*

NZ Rugby Museum

NZ Rugby Museum

Don Wright (left) and Jimmy Mill.

Herald, he dismissed it as 'the weakest team New Zealand has ever had: weak in scrums, weak on defence and lacking in pace'.

Tyler, who clearly hadn't heard of the unspoken rule that All Blacks don't criticise their own, boasted that the team of which he was a member conceded only eight tries in 31 matches while the 1924 team had let in 11 in just five matches. He then turned to specific selections, going through player by player, position by position. 'But the greatest injustice of all is the exclusion of Wright. He undoubtedly is the best halfback in the Dominion and is the ideal type.'

Don Wright had a good game at halfback for Auckland against the All Blacks, especially by comparison with his All Black counterpart, Jimmy Mill, who by most accounts had not played to his usual high standard in either Australia or Auckland. There were extenuating circumstances for the All Blacks. They played within 14 hours of landing ashore and, as lock Read Masters noted, 'We could still feel the roll of the good ship *Manuka* when the ball was played for the kick-off and knew that it would not take a very strong team to beat us.'

The loss, though, led to a growing clamour, especially from Auckland, for the inclusion of Wright in the touring squad. It was lent encouragement by the manager of the team in Australia, Ernie Little, a Wellingtonian, who had cabled the New Zealand union after the Auckland loss suggesting another back be added.

The Auckland match was on a Wednesday, the Manawatu-Horowhenua match on the following Saturday, and the team was leaving Wellington on the Tuesday after that, so clearly time was against the campaigners for change.

The match in Palmerston North went ahead — the All Blacks won 27–12 — but the New Zealand union remained publicly quiet about whether another player would be added. There was plenty going on behind the scenes, though.

On the Friday before the match, a group of what was later described as 'certain gentlemen in Wellington' went to Coates in his office in Parliament. The import and clandestine nature of the meeting may be gauged by the fact that it was at 10.30 pm they went calling on the deputy prime minister.

They asked Coates to seek out the New Zealand union management committee the next day in Palmerston North and suggest to these worthies that Wright be added to the touring party. Coates was told Auckland citizens would pay whatever was necessary to get Wright away, though whether Auckland citizens knew this was never made clear.

The extra payment would have been necessary because the English union, which was organising the whole of the British tour, had agreed to pay for only 29 players.

Coates did as he was bid and the management committee duly met in Palmerston North after the game, though some of the national selectors — among them the chairman of the selection panel and dominant personality Ted McKenzie — knew nothing about it.

Reporters sniffing around were told little, but they knew something was

Ron Palenski Collection

One of the election posters for Gordon Coates in 1925, the year he became prime minister and the year after he tried to change the All Black selectors' minds.

going on. 'Rumour was busy all day yesterday,' the *Dominion* reported on the Monday morning. Among the rumours was one that Wright was told to get himself post-haste on the Main Trunk express to Wellington.

The New Zealand union chairman, Stan Dean, who was also manager of the team leaving on the Tuesday, eventually broke the official silence on the Sunday night:

> A communication has been received from Mr Little, as manager of the All Blacks on their Australian tour, suggesting the inclusion of an extra player. This communication has been sent on to the selection committee and will be further considered at a meeting of the management committee to be held tomorrow.

The *Dominion* reporter, who was not identified by either name or pseudonym, remarked in rather an understatement that the situation was getting very complicated — especially considering the team was leaving within hours of the newly scheduled management committee meeting.

He was not as confident as Aucklanders that if a player were added, it would be Wright.

He thought that 'Ginger' Nicholls, who was going with the team as a journalist anyway, would have equal claim, as would a Canterbury halfback, Clarrie St George.

'If Wright is chosen, Wellington will be dissatisfied,' he wrote. 'If Nicholls is chosen, Auckland will be dissatisfied; if St George is chosen, the North Island will be dissatisfied.'

Wright's supporters said he would be the natural halfback to put inside Auckland backs Ces Badeley, Bert Cooke and Fred Lucas, all of whom were in the team for Britain and accustomed to Wright's play. But a similar argument could be put for Nicholls, whose brother Mark was the chosen first five-eighths in the team.

It was against this background that the New Zealand union management committee met, at virtually the eleventh hour, to consider what should be done. It was not a happy meeting. It was, perhaps surprisingly, open to the press and the *Dominion* on the Tuesday morning said 'the most strained relations that have existed for many years in the controlling body of the New Zealand rugby game were evident at the meeting'.

The meeting degenerated as soon as the minutes of the previous meeting — that held in Palmerston North on the Saturday night — were read. They said the meeting had been called 'as a result of representations by the Hon.

The manager of the Invincibles and one of the most powerful figures in rugby history, Stan Dean.

J. G. Coates in connection with an offer from Auckland on behalf of the citizens of that town to subscribe £500 for the expense of D. Wright, if he were selected'.

The minutes then said: 'The selectors who had been consulted had turned down the proposal to select Wright.'

Dean, who as chairman of the union and team manager was crucial to the whole process, then left the meeting so he could attend a series of farewells for the team in various venues in Wellington: one was a parliamentary farewell, one by the Wellington City Council and a farewell dinner hosted by Dean himself.

A Wellington member of the management committee, Dolph Kitto, was left in charge, and he was not happy because neither he nor the chief selector, Ted McKenzie, had been privy to the meeting held in Palmerston North. Neither had the Canterbury delegate, Jim Fletcher, who said the meeting should never have been held.

The union's treasurer, Edgar Wylie, was left to argue the official position,

185

such as it was. He said the Palmerston North meeting had been held because of 'a very urgent appeal from the north' and because representations had been made by the prime minister.

Kitto asked at whose instigation the meeting was held.

Wylie: Mr Coates and the prime minister.

Kitto: What have Mr Coates and the prime minister got to do with it?

McKenzie: They may be good at politics, but they may have to improve themselves at football.

Wylie: The position is that Mr Massey is entitled to consideration.

McKenzie: In politics, certainly.

Wylie: In politics or anything else.

McKenzie: That is not your sincere opinion, Mr Wylie?

Wylie: It is.

McKenzie: Not with regard to football?

Wylie: Whether or not we agree, I think a man in his position or Mr Holland's is entitled to respect. [Harry Holland was then leader of the Labour Party.]

The discussion then moved on to the niceties about whether the eight national selectors had been consulted on the Saturday night about Wright and, if they had, whether they agreed.

Wylie argued some selectors were in favour of adding Wright but McKenzie disagreed, saying that only one was. One of the selectors, Harry Davis from Canterbury, had been quoted two days previously as saying he had received a recommendation from the management committee that Wright be added.

McKenzie accused Wylie and other committee members of trying to curry favour with Auckland and he told Wylie he did not know what he was talking about. Wylie responded by saying the press should be excluded from the meeting.

McKenzie: 'I want it in the open. I want the people of New Zealand to see how things have been carried on.'

The meeting eventually ended with a motion of confidence in the team as selected.

Wright never went to Britain. He did play for the All Blacks, though, going to Australia in 1925 with a team that did not include any of the Invincibles. He played in seven of the eight matches, including both of the unofficial tests against New South Wales.

The day after the Invincibles left for Britain, Coates made a formal statement in which he said he delivered a message to the management committee as requested 'without any embellishments or qualifications'. He said the prime minister knew nothing about it. He then added a sentence which would have echoes down the rugby years: 'Personally, it is unnecessary for me to remark that I hold very strong views that the management of sport should be entirely free from any political or government control, and that it should be left entirely to those who have been elected for that purpose.'

Massey died in May of 1925 and Coates became prime minister three weeks later. The Reform Party under Coates — with the slogan that he was 'the man who gets things done' — was returned to power in the general election in November 1925.

The All Blacks, for all the misgivings about them before they left, were unbeaten and earned the title, the Invincibles.

The Case for Neutrality

Of all the frightful decisions, real and imagined, made by referees in New Zealand test matches, none has been written or talked about as much as that by John Dallas of Scotland against Wales in 1905. But that's a hand-me-down story, one drawn out over time and embellished according to the nationality of who is relating the story.

There's a much more recent example of the All Blacks being wronged in a test by a referee and it adds hugely to the credence of the story that people with feet in both camps acknowledged the wrong.

The outline of the story is still recent enough that it remains relatively fresh in the memories and lies like a cancer in the soul of those who were affected by it: the All Blacks in South Africa in 1976.

South Africa had won the first and third tests and New Zealand the second, meaning the All Blacks had to win the fourth at Ellis Park in Johannesburg to square the series.

Fourteen minutes into the second half, the Springboks were ahead by a point, 12–11. The All Black wing, Bryan Williams, used his speed and sidestep to make space wide out and he ran and centre-kicked. Flanker Kevin Eveleigh anticipated, scooped the ball up, then threw a long pass to the All Black centre, Bruce Robertson. It seemed for a moment — to the 75,000 packed into the ground and to the untold hundreds of thousands watching on television — that Robertson may have had the pace to get across in the corner. But the South African fullback, Ian Robertson, had the better angle and had his namesake covered. Bruce Robertson could see plan B was needed and, as he could do very well, he slipped in a little kick ahead. The ball sat up over the goal-line as was intended but Bruce Robertson never got to it because he was obstructed by the other Robertson.

The referee, Gert Bezuidenhout, clearly saw what happened because he blew his whistle and gave the All Blacks a penalty, which Williams turned into three points and New Zealand regained the lead, 14–12.

But the lead regained should have been 17–12. Rather than a penalty, Bezuidenhout should have given the All Blacks a penalty try (tries then were worth four points). The All Black captain, Andy Leslie, demanded it. So did other All Blacks in the vicinity, showing a little less diplomacy and tact than Leslie. So did any New Zealander anywhere watching. But it wasn't just New Zealanders who saw the injustice.

Up in the official area of the main stand, an area known as the glasshouse, the all-powerful president of the South African Rugby Board, Danie Craven,

South African wing Gerrie Germishuys gains the attention of All Black first five-eighth Doug Bruce and second-five Joe Morgan during the 1976 series.

Ron Palenski Collection

The man who was robbed of a try in South Africa, Bruce Robertson.

turned to the manager of the All Blacks, Noel Stanley, and said, 'Noel, that was a try. I am very sorry. It was a wrong decision.'

The prime minister of South Africa, the forbiddingly white Johannes Vorster, was not given much to outward shows of emotion. He too was in the glasshouse. According to Stanley, Vorster expressively shook his head from side to side in a clear indication he did not agree with Bezuidenhout either. 'There's no doubt Vorster knew his rugby,' Stanley later recalled. 'I found him a very knowledgeable chap.'

The All Blacks clung to their two-point lead until 10 minutes to go when the Springboks' first five-eighths, Gerald Bosch, kicked his second penalty goal of the afternoon, this one as a result of Bezuidenhout finding fault with the way the All Black prop, Bill Bush, dealt with the Springboks' main lineout jumper, Kevin de Klerk. The South Africans lifted their jumpers — lifting in lineouts was not legal until 1997 — and the All Blacks, and other opponents including the Lions of two years before, had to find ways to counter that. The most effective way was to take out the lifters. But that's another story.

So the All Blacks lost the fourth test 15–14 and lost the series 3–1. They should have won the test and drawn the series.

Craven, not always the friend of New Zealand he pretended to be, again referred to the Bezuidenhout decision when he spoke at a reception for both teams the night of the test. 'If ever there was a penalty try, that was one,' he said. 'I watched it again on television and I have no doubt that there should have been a penalty try.' (The ability to see a replay on television was a novelty in itself. Television was introduced in South Africa only the year before.)

The long and bitter reaction to Bezuidenhout's incompetence — for that was what it was — was exacerbated by the whole background to the tour. The All Blacks went there with a sizeable proportion of their fellow citizens not wanting them to go at all; but they went with an equally sizeable proportion willing them on to at last beat the South Africans on their own turf. It was much more than a rugby tour. Countries to which rugby was a foreign or unknown concept didn't want the All Blacks there either and at the Olympic Games in Montreal, African, Asian and Caribbean countries pulled out in protest. For going through that much, the All Blacks — New Zealand — could at least have expected competent officiating of their matches.

The fourth test and the obstruction of Robertson was the most blatant example, but there were others. The All Blacks argued that a wrong decision in the first test by referee Ian Gourlay could have cost them the match; Bezuidenhout ruled out a penalty kick by Sid Going in the third test because he said he took too long to take it.

But there is always spilt milk after rugby tests and no amount of crying can ever reverse the result. The All Blacks were not blameless and maybe decisions made by coaches and selectors cost them the series anyway: the lack of a specialist goal-kicker, for one, the lack of a specialist fullback up to the rigorous demands of test rugby in South Africa for another; deficiencies in the tight forwards another.

It is easier to point unequivocally to a wrong decision by a referee than to somehow blame the cumulative effects of selection or coaching errors or player mistakes.

'We wuz robbed' is the oldest, most repetitive cry in sport. The All Blacks were robbed in the fourth test. They were robbed in the series. But by whom?

Rather than blame the referees, blame those responsible for putting referees in the position where their lack of experience or ability could cost one or other side a match, particularly a match in a series on which so much rested, a series that was always going to have white-hot tension.

The blame in this case should rest not so much with the South Africans, but with the New Zealand Rugby Union. The union had the chance to seek neutral referees, but chose not to take it. 'Neutral referees' is now a common enough expression, but it is not explicit enough. Any referee should be neutral by definition. What is meant by the phrase 'neutral referees' is third country referees, that is, referees from a country other than those involved in the game.

The principle of third country referees was well established by 1976, just not in South Africa or New Zealand. It had been the norm in Britain since early in the 20th century and All Black, Springbok or Wallaby teams have never played a test in Britain without a third country referee. But travel and cost in what was then an amateur sport probably worked against the principle extending around the world. It has always been a simple matter for referees in Britain to hop on a train and be whisked off to London or Cardiff or Edinburgh or wherever; less easy to travel around the world. Such was the weight attached to test series, though, and such were the financial benefits to the unions if not the players, that it became imperative for third country referees to be appointed everywhere.

Stanley had a press conference in Johannesburg the day after the debacle at Ellis Park. He was asked by John Reason of the *Daily Telegraph* in London — Reason being well aware of the principle of third country referees — if New Zealand had agreed to the series being controlled by South African referees.

Stanley, a Taranaki dairy farmer who was a member of the New Zealand Rugby Union's ruling council, replied that South Africa had offered 'neutral' referees but the council had declined the offer. Stanley did not respond to suggestions that the decision had been made in secret and never made public — not that he needed to. Any number of decisions made by the supreme New Zealand rugby authority were made in secret and never made public.

Quite naturally, reporters on the tour and in New Zealand saw this as a sensational admission by the New Zealand union. The taint of villainy quickly switched from the unfortunate Bezuidenhout to the New Zealand union and its chairman, Jack Sullivan, an affable but serious man who had a reputation, not wholly undeserved, for saying 'no comment' to anything remotely contentious.

It emerged that the offer of third country referees may have been made by Craven to Sullivan, or perhaps to his deputy, Ces Blazey, at an International

Rugby Board meeting in March of 1976, or possibly at the equivalent meeting the year before, in March of 1975. Details were as sketchy as that. Sullivan, true to his image, would not comment other than to say it was not his union's policy to seek or request neutral referees on an overseas tour. Blazey was apparently not asked.

There is no written record of the offer being made at either of those meetings but that does not necessarily mean it was not made. If it was intended to be merely a bilateral agreement, between New Zealand and South Africa, the subject could have been broached at any stage — in a bar, in a restaurant, in an airport lounge. If it was merely a verbal offer, as is likely, there would be no written record.

Sullivan and Craven went back a long way. They were opponents on the field in New Zealand in 1937; in the tempestuous series of 1956 in New Zealand, Craven was the Springboks' manager and Sullivan the coach of the All Blacks both then and again in 1960 in South Africa. They knew each other well; they socialised together, they exchanged Christmas greetings; their wives shopped together. Blazey, although with neither the playing nor the coaching background, was of a similar age and had great respect within the international rugby community for his administrative ability.

It is entirely possible that at either the 1975 or 1976 IRB meetings, probably the former given time constraints that would have applied if the decision had been left to 1976, the three men had a casual conversation about referees and decided no change was necessary. Sullivan would have taken Craven at his word, as would Blazey at that stage. It was only later, in the mid-1980s, that there was a falling out between Blazey and Craven, caused principally by Craven's less than open declarations about what he knew, or did not know, about the rebel All Black tour of 1986.

This was also a time when the International Rugby Board was an even more reactionary creature than it is now and it seldom imposed its collective will on anyone or anything. A decision on neutral referees would have been made then by the countries involved, not by the IRB.

Not long after the All Blacks returned from South Africa in 1976, the New Zealand union council met. The format for its meetings then was that they would be 'open' for perhaps the first hour or so, when one agenda would be traversed and reporters could be present. Discussions in this section of the meeting were generally, though not always, of a non-controversial nature. If a councillor felt strongly enough about something, or wanted to get his name in the paper, he could risk the wrath of Sullivan by saying something contentious.

When the reporters were asked to leave, the council got down to its other agenda, the serious business. These meetings could last for hours, at the end of which the chairman and the secretary (in 1976 it was Jack Jeffs) would call back the reporters and tell them what the council had agreed they should be told, which was never everything that had been discussed.

It was after this meeting in Auckland in 1976 that Sullivan said it was not the policy of the union to seek neutral referees, but ... There was always a but after such meetings.

The meeting was in Auckland rather than Wellington because councillors were there to farewell the second New Zealand team of 1976. This comprised players who had not been to South Africa and they were leaving on a pioneering tour of Uruguay and Argentina.

These new All Blacks (only Andy Haden, John Callesen, Peter Sloane and Ian Stevens had been All Blacks before) found when they were in Argentina that the two unofficial tests against the Pumas would be refereed by a 'neutral', Michel Messan of France. This had apparently been arranged by the Argentine union without reference to New Zealand and, such was the indifferent quality of the Argentine referees who controlled the other matches, no one had any objection.

The era of hometown refereeing was drawing to a close, with or without the approval of the New Zealand union. One of the reasons New Zealand did not pursue the principle of third country referees with any vigour was to protect their own referees, as misguided as that may have been. The council reasoned that if referees from somewhere else came to New Zealand to take charge of tests, it would be unfair on New Zealand referees who would be denied test opportunities. This gradually changed only when the British countries agreed reluctantly to accept New Zealand referees for matches there. Tom Doocey of Christchurch became the first New Zealander to referee Five (now Six) Nations matches when he had charge of England–Scotland and France–Wales in 1983.

Whatever the New Zealand union's misgivings, change was being forced. France had toured New Zealand twice, in 1961 and 1968, and played tests with New Zealand referees but when negotiations began for a third tour, in 1979, the French said New Zealand referees would not be good enough any more.

The head of the French Rugby Federation was Albert Ferrasse, a man for whom democracy was a Greek word and not easily translated into French. He told Blazey that France would go to New Zealand in 1979 only if the referees came from somewhere else. Blazey, whose lucid thoughts on rugby included being able to see writing on walls, acquiesced and an Irishman well known to the All Blacks, John West, took charge of the two 1979 tests.

That pretty much brought to an end the era of hometown refs. Australia held out for another four years but by the time of the 1983 Bledisloe Cup match in Sydney, it too had bowed to the inevitable. A New Zealand referee had one final fling in charge of an All Black test when Dave Bishop took control of the second of the matches against a World XV in the New Zealand union centenary series in 1992.

The much-criticised Bezuidenhout was the last South African to referee a test between the All Blacks and the Springboks.

Of the 13 penalty tries given the All Blacks in tests, two have been against South Africa, one in 2001 and the other in 2002.

Originals in High Demand

The Original All Blacks of 1905–06 had had enough of playing as the end of their tour neared. They played 32 matches in Britain and Ireland between mid-September and the end of December. On New Year's Day they played France and, against their wishes, they were then dispatched to the United States for another three games (the first of them a virtual exhibition but a game nevertheless).

The *Otago Witness* reported in mid-December 1905:

> From private letters received in Dunedin by the latest English mail, it would appear that several members of the New Zealand team were heartily sick of the constant travelling from one town to another. They express themselves tired of the tour and anxious to get home again. Many of them are suffering from minor ailments, consequent on the change of climate, and complain of the severe cold of the English winter.

Yet for all their gruelling programme, there were still plans for them to play more.

It is not generally recalled in later accounts of the tour that there was an official move for them to play a combined British side — an embryonic Lions team — as a grand finale to the tour (and for those British people who supported the idea, a chance for more than just the Welsh to taste victory against these upstart colonials).

197

The first move for that match came towards the end of November —
about three weeks before the All Blacks' denouement in Cardiff — when
the New Zealand union management committee meeting in Wellington,
buoyed by the success of the team thus far, cabled the manager, George
Dixon, and told him to sort out another game.

The game was suggested for January 6, a week after the final scheduled
match against Swansea, and rather than add more to the New Zealand union
coffers, it was proposed that proceeds go to the King's Hospital Fund.

The game, it was thought, would ideally be against a combined British
team, seen as a fitting climax to the tour.

Even before the test against Wales, a proposed 'United Kingdom XV' was
published in British newspapers: at fullback was George Davies of Swansea,
who did not play in the test against the All Blacks and had last played for
Wales in 1900. The threequarters were Ted Morgan and Gwyn Nicholls of
Wales, who both played in the Welsh test, the latter as captain, Alec Timms
or Lewis Macleod of Scotland and Basil Maclear of Ireland. The halfbacks
were Ernest Simson of Scotland and Dicky Owens of Wales. The forwards
were listed as Robert Stronach (Scotland), Arthur Harding (Wales), Charles
Hammond (England), Alf Tedford (Ireland), Joseph Wallace (Ireland),
Charles Newbold (England), Joseph Hodges (Wales) and Hugh Monteith
(Scotland).

On what basis the team was chosen or by whom was not recorded but it
was a curious selection because as well as the fullback, Davies, several did not
play for their national teams against the All Blacks. Monteith was chosen
for Scotland to meet the All Blacks in their first test, but had to withdraw
because of injury.

The match fell through in the week before the Welsh test, though, when
the Welsh Rugby Union decided the proposed date of January 6 was too
close to its scheduled match against England in the opening round of what
was then grandly known as the international rugby championship (now
more prosaically the Six Nations). That game was played at Richmond in

How the Auckland weekly newspaper, the *Observer*, marked the exit of 1905 and the entrance of 1906.

Southwest London on January 13 and Wales beat England 16–3. As an aside, it reflected the influence the New Zealanders had had. Wales fielded a wing forward, Cliff Pritchard, but they called him a rover to avoid accusations of hypocrisy after the trenchant time they gave the All Blacks' wing forward, Dave Gallaher, in Wales. England, reflecting the five-try drubbing at the hands of the All Blacks, fielded 10 new caps.

With Wales out of the combined team, the English union dropped the idea.

Another suggested addition to the All Blacks' programme came from a former All Black, William McKenzie, a journalist who was better known as 'Offside Mac' for his borderline wing forward play during the 1890s.

Writing in the *Evening Post* in Wellington after the loss in Cardiff, he came out with all guns blazing for a return match against Wales.

He said footballers and the football-loving public have been waiting anxiously for a return fixture to be announced.

Neither the New Zealand union nor the team has made any move in the matter and we can only come to the conclusion that each is prepared to abide by the beating administered on December 16 and surrender our right to the title of champion. In other words, each is taking the licking lying down.

McKenzie argued he was not being greedy but felt at least one other match was necessary to determine which was the better side.

'Then if Wales can win, we can cheerfully admit that she has the better men; if she is beaten, then we should play a third test. It must be one thing or another.'

McKenzie's idea of a series to determine a winner was not new to rugby; series had been played in New Zealand, Australia and South Africa during tours, but not in Britain.

His plea was published 12 days after the All Blacks were beaten 3–0 but before detailed reports of the match had arrived in New Zealand. Only brief, cabled reports had been published by then and it was not until late in January that New Zealand readers were able to learn in detail of what happened in Cardiff on December 16.

McKenzie had a crack at determining the reason for the loss: 'Until there is further information supplied, one cannot but come to the conclusion that the beating by Wales was the result of mismanagement by our side as much as our bad play.'

He thought even then that a Welshman had refereed the match. 'If this is so, it only proves the disingenuous impartiality of the New Zealanders. If they allowed a Welshman to referee in that match they deserved their defeat.' (The referee, as doleful history records, was a Scot, John Dallas).

The editor of the *Evening Post* was inundated with letters about McKenzie's article, so many that the newspaper apologised for not being able to print them all. McKenzie's article had not been greeted warmly.

'Offside Mac must, with others, accept the defeat in a sportsmanlike spirit and not call for another match,' one correspondent said.

Another said New Zealand were not disgraced by the loss. 'Practically as much credit redounds to a defeated side which can take its beating in good part as to its conquerors. Too much feeling has, perhaps, been imparted into these matches but we must give praise where praise is due.'

In comments which were a portent of accusations of arrogance and a lack of humility against New Zealand many years later, a letter writer who signed himself 'Sense and Absurdity' wanted to know 'what divine right New Zealanders possess over any other sportsmen in the world that the present order of things should be reversed for their benefit?'

Another writer, this one of clear Welsh origins because he signed himself 'Cymru Ambydd', thought that New Zealand might be able to teach English rugby something 'but Wales has nothing to learn from her. Rugby is the Welshman's game and who can gainsay it? . . . [B]e a sport and take your beating like a man.'

McKenzie, by this time beleaguered, returned to the fray in early 1906. 'As a footballer, I was prepared to admit that on the day's play honours rested with Wales, but at the same time I wanted more proof that their football was really superior to ours,' he wrote.

By this time better informed about the match and who played in it, McKenzie justified his earlier mismanagement comment by saying the star backs in the New Zealand team had been played out in earlier matches and as a result of them 'cracking up', lesser lights had to be fielded against Wales. The absence of the wing, George Smith, was a calamity, he said. (Smith missed the Welsh match because of a broken collar bone.)

He also dismissed the proposition that Wales had nothing to learn from New Zealand. He said the Welsh adopted several New Zealand practices, including fielding Pritchard as a wing forward.

He then borrowed the cricket example to justify his stance. 'In cricket, Australia play a series of tests with England and no one makes any charges of unsportsmanlike actions regarding the playing of these matches. On the contrary, they are accepted, are looked for and are evidence of true sport.'

Another suggestion, floated from time to time, to add to the workload of the All Blacks was a game against the Northern Union, the forerunner of the Rugby Football League in Britain. The strength of British rugby had been split in two 10 years before when the majority of clubs in Yorkshire and Lancashire seceded from the English union to form the Northern Union. The root cause was that the working men of the north wanted to be paid compensation for taking time off work to play rugby; the middle class dominance of southern England was opposed to any form of professionalism, as they called it, and English rugby took years to recover.

When the Original All Blacks were in Britain, English rugby was still at a low ebb and there were arguments in British newspapers that a fairer test for the All Blacks would be to play Northern Union teams which were by then playing the evolving game of rugby league.

The third branch of football then was soccer, and the president of the

Football League, J. J. Bentley, wrote that the Northern Union would give a much better account of itself against the All Blacks than the RFU clubs the New Zealanders were playing.

But anyone who understood the amateur ethic that dominated rugby for a century knew that such a match would have been an impossibility. Any All Black who appeared on the same field as a rugby league player would have immediately been banned for life.

The Rugby Football Union dismissed any chance of such a game and it was never seriously pursued by the All Black manager, George Dixon. Some of the All Blacks had been interested in such a game and they got their chance 18 months after the tour when they joined the newly-formed New Zealand league team, sometimes known as 'the professional All Blacks' and sometimes as the 'All Golds'.

Rugby and the Republic

In the totality of rugby history, only one country goes close to matching the All Blacks' overall record. The South Africans have been New Zealand's perennial foes — they played in the amateur days for a mythical 'world championship' and ascendancy was never with one side or the other for long. Wales had a particular rivalry for much of the 20th century and Australia have been the most frequent opponents, but matches between the All Blacks and the Springboks were the ultimate event.

Statistics bear this out. The All Blacks' overall test record at the start of 2008 was a winning percentage of 74.1, far and away better than any other national rugby team. Against Wales, the All Blacks' record of success was 86.9 per cent and against Australia, 66.4 per cent. But the lowest All Black winning percentage against one country was 55.5 per cent against South Africa — and for much of the 20th century that figure hovered around 50 per cent or lower.

With the intensity of the rugby rivalry came the baggage of South Africa's racial attitude. Until reunification in 1992, the white South African treatment of non-whites dominated the rugby connection, scarring New Zealand in the process, and there has been no deeper or longer-lasting disfiguring mark on New Zealand's record than the tour by South Africa in 1981.

The issue reached its apogee in the 1980s with first the 1981 tour, then the failed attempt by New Zealand to send a team there in 1985 and finally the rebel tour by All Blacks in 1986.

In purely a sporting sense, New Zealand rugby was obsessed with South Africa because they were so good and the game and its results meant as much there as they did in New Zealand. The longer New Zealand went without success in South Africa, the deeper the obsession. Only with the abolition of apartheid, the success by John Hart's All Blacks in 1996 and the full advent of professionalism did that obsession mellow.

Now, South African players are as familiar in New Zealand as they are in their own land.

The depth of the New Zealand obsession, and now familiarity, with South Africa has even led to a curious quirk in the use of language. In the news media particularly, it has become almost a cliché for New Zealanders to use 'the republic' as a synonym for South Africa. A television newsreader might say, 'The All Blacks left the republic today . . .' The curiosity is that this linguistic device is not used in relation to any other country. 'The republic' is never used if the All Blacks are leaving France or Ireland or Italy or the United States or Argentina or any other of the republics in which they have played. Only South Africa.

And only South Africa has ever regularly dictated to New Zealand who should be in All Black teams: not on the basis of merit, but on the basis of colour. It is well enough known that the first All Blacks to visit South Africa in 1928 were deprived of the services of George Nepia and Jimmy Mill; the 1949 team would in a fair world surely have included at least Johnny Smith and Vince Bevan and perhaps Ben Couch; the 1960 team may have included Pat Walsh or Stan Hill. Only by 1970 did New Zealand put its foot down and say emphatically that enough was enough (and even that took negotiations over several years).

Such dictation did not begin with the All Blacks in 1928, though. Apartheid as an institutionalised and legalised form of racial discrimination did not begin until the election of the Nationalist Government in 1948, but there was unofficial and widespread assumed white supremacy before that.

The first New Zealand rugby contact with South Africa came during the Boer War between 1899 and 1902 when Britain and its empire fought against the independence of Transvaal and Orange Free State. New Zealand soldiers' diaries record scratch rugby matches either among themselves or against British units. One of the Boer commanders even agreed towards the end of the war to a ceasefire so his forces and British soldiers could meet in a rugby match. It never took place, but it was the thought that counted.

Many New Zealanders stayed in South Africa after the war and in Durban a club of them dominated rugby there for a time, winning the Murray Cup, open to all senior teams in Natal, four years in a row. Even the official history of South African rugby acknowledged that the New Zealanders did much to make rugby popular in Natal, where soccer had previously been the sport of choice.

One of the great figures of New Zealand rugby, Dave Gallaher, the captain of the All Blacks in 1905–06, fought in the Boer War but there is no record he ever played there (although it is likely that he did).

Gallaher and his vice-captain, Billy Stead, recorded in the book they wrote after the Originals' tour that the prospects of rugby in South Africa were excellent. 'It does not seem possible to imagine a game that is more suited to the climate and conditions of that country or to the habits and temperament of the people who occupy it,' they wrote. 'There is something about the climate and the country that makes one feel instinctively that here is a place where rugby football would thrive if it would anywhere in the world.'

The storm clouds on South Africa's rugby horizon were racial and New Zealanders were among the first to feel their effects.

After the First World War a range of sports events were organised in Britain and France to keep troops occupied while they were waiting for ships home. Among them was a King's Cup rugby tournament which was won by New Zealand and one of the outstanding players for the team was a Wellingtonian of part-Caribbean extraction, Nathaniel Wilson (although because of his colour he was forever known as 'Ranji', after the cricketer, Kumar Ranjitsinhji, an Indian aristocrat who played for England).

Ron Palenski Collection

King George V presents the New Zealand Services team captain, Jim Ryan, with the King's Cup at the end of the 1919 tournament.

Wilson had played 21 times for New Zealand, including 10 tests, between 1908 and 1914 and was widely regarded as the leading New Zealand loose forward, a sort of Josh Kronfeld or Richie McCaw of his day.

The Australian army team, which incidentally was the only team to beat the New Zealanders in the six-match King's Cup, called in to Cape Town on the way home. A match against the locals was offered but had to be turned down because the rugby season had not then started. This got the South African Rugby Board thinking, though, and in early April 1919 it sent a cable to the South African high commissioner in London suggesting he ask the New Zealand team to break its homeward journey for a short tour.

The high commissioner was the right man to ask. He was William Philip Schreiner — better known as W. P. Schreiner — a noted lawyer and politician who was also president of the South African board until he was sent to London at the start of the war. He made contact with New Zealand authorities, the tour was organised and Schreiner in mid-May cabled Cape Town that a team of 29 New Zealand servicemen would be arriving for a three-week tour at about the end of the month.

But then it got ugly, as South African rugby historian Gideon Nieman discovered. He wrote:

> On the same day that Schreiner thought that he had completed his negotiations successfully, the rugby board met in Cape Town. It had suddenly dawned upon the board that a New Zealand Services team might include Maoris. After a heated discussion, the board decided with eight votes to six to send the following cable to the high commissioner: Confidential stop if visitors include Maoris tour would be wrecked and immense harm politically and otherwise would follow stop please explain position fully and try to arrange exclusion stop and ends.

As Nieman recorded, one of the ironies was that one of Schreiner's sons, W. F. R. (Bill) Schreiner (later a Springbok selector), seconded the motion to send the fateful cable.

It therefore fell to the older Schreiner in London to tell the New Zealand authorities that Wilson — who was not Maori but whose complexion reflected his mother's Caribbean origins — was not welcome in South Africa.

Schreiner was the least likely possible person to send such a message. Almost alone among South African politicians, he argued for full and equal rights for the black and coloured population and specifically the right to vote and the right to be elected to parliament. He had been prime minister of Cape Colony but resigned at the start of the Boer War. He returned to politics when South Africa was united in 1910 and was offered a seat in the Senate, according to one obituary, 'on the ground of thorough acquaintance with the reasonable wants and wishes of the coloured races'.

Schreiner died three weeks after having to pass on the message that Wilson was not wanted. *The Times* in its obituary said of him: 'It would be cynical to say that he was too honest to be a great success as a politician; but there would be an element of truth in it nevertheless.'

The New Zealand army team, which included 15 who were or would be All Blacks, went ahead with its tour and won 11 of its 15 matches. Among the losses was to Griqualand West at Kimberley, but the New Zealanders did not leave empty-handed. Each player was presented with a medallion of South African gold inset with a diamond from the Kimberley mines (the first but certainly not the last time

The flanker the South Africans didn't want, 'Ranji' Wilson.

New Zealand rugby players came home bearing gifts). That evidently was not their only material benefit from the tour. The players were short on cash when they arrived in Cape Town but Ted Shaw, a New Zealand jockey riding in South Africa, made himself known to them and offered them a few tips. With the New Zealanders present and punting, Shaw rode three winners in one day.

The army team reassembled in 1920 for a match against Wellington and, in a nice touch, included Wilson in the line-up.

In a book about one of the army players, Alex Bruce, Bob Luxford (who runs the New Zealand Rugby Museum in Palmerston North) wrote that Bruce's son Don recalled his father felt guilty about Wilson's omission from the tour, feeling that 'both team and management had taken the soft option — that a stand then on the racial issue of coloured inclusion would have saved humiliation of a fine man and sportsman and set the stage for later tour consideration'.

In other words, a New Zealand stand against South African racism in

1919 could have spared later generations a great deal of heartache, heartbreak and outrage.

There is an unproven, and probably unprovable, suspicion that 1919 was not the only time Wilson was left out of a team because of his colour. In 1913, with a New Zealand tour of California looming, Wilson was one of the most dominant players in the country and captained the North Island. Yet he was not chosen in the team to tour and it has been speculated occasionally since that he was left out because American attitudes toward non-whites then were not much better than South Africans'.

The story is lent some credence by the fact that New Zealand had not then played test rugby for three years and the team for California had only four players with previous test experience. Yet one who did, Wilson, was not chosen, although after the team left for California, he played two tests for a second-choice All Black team against Australia.

An indication of American attitudes to non-whites appeared in one of the Californian newspaper reports about the All Blacks. The players were due to visit the Reno Press Club when they were in Nevada for their match against the state university side. During a discussion at the club about issuing invitations to the players, one member objected on the grounds that they were all blacks.

'I don't give a damn if they are niggers,' was the reported reply. 'They are footballers and they are coming here.'

The army tour and the racially motivated exclusion of Wilson thus began the well-trodden trail through the 20th century of sport, politics and protest: intensity on the field and off it. Opinions were polarised and while one side lamented the inadequacies of hometown refereeing and itineraries arranged to favour the home side, an increasing number throughout the 1960s and 1970s lamented that the tours even occurred.

The New Zealand union tried to make gradual changes to the South African tour conditions. It successfully sought agreement from the International Rugby Board in 1962 that future New Zealand teams going to

South Africa could include Maori (assuming the All Black selectors agreed). South Africa remained unbending and at the annual meeting of the IRB in March of 1966, chairman Danie Craven — the chairmanship then was taken in turns and it happened to be South Africa's — said the 1962 agreement could not be fulfilled. The IRB minutes record:

> Dr Craven explained that unfortunately the intention stated in minute 10 of board meeting of the 16th of March 1962 that Maoris could be included in future New Zealand teams visiting South Africa could not be fulfilled at this time, notwithstanding the unanimous wish of the South African Rugby Board.

New Zealand thus cancelled the tour and went to Britain in 1967 instead. By 1970, though, a minor crack had appeared in the South African racial armour and, for the first time, three Maori and one Samoan were in the All Black team that toured. But that, the critics argued, was pandering to apartheid and not calculated to bring about its downfall.

Rugby and New Zealand became the catalyst for worldwide protest against giving what was interpreted as support to the South African apartheid regime. New Zealand became the focal point at the Olympic Games in Montreal in 1976 when about 30 African, Caribbean and Asian countries either withdrew or did not arrive because of the presence of the All Blacks in South Africa. A Scottish golfing resort, Gleneagles, became a name mixed up in the argument of sporting contacts with South Africa because it was there in 1977 that some Commonwealth heads of government attempted to hammer out an agreement that would be acceptable to all. It never was.

The New Zealand Rugby Football Union, charged with the promotion of the game, became the hero for those who continued to support playing against South Africa and the villain for those who opposed. The union steadfastly maintained that its sole concern was rugby and such matters as the domestic politics of another country, or even their own country's foreign affairs, were not its concern. Sport and politics, the argument wearily went, should never mix though they had been through the blender since the start of the century.

Publicly, the New Zealand union was resolute. Privately, some of its administrators began to have doubts. (Though not all because, even as late as December 2007, the administrator most identified with pursuing contacts with South Africa, Ron Don, was given a service award by the NZRU and in his acceptance speech he blamed, as he always used to, the news media for rugby's ills.)

It was ironic then that it was Don's union, Auckland, which significantly opposed the sending of a New Zealand team to South Africa in 1985. Auckland were then chaired by Don's successor, Malcolm Dick, who had played in South Africa with the 1970 team. 'Auckland is convinced that no real good can come from the tour proceeding,' Dick said in a letter to the NZRFU and all provincial unions.

The New Zealand union went ahead with planning for the tour — 'accepting the invitation' was the standard phrase — but it is now known that the union's governing council, for probably the first time in relation to South African issues, was not wholly in favour. After a series of meetings with the Labour Government, the council met on April 17, 1985 for the tour decision. After it was moved that the invitation be accepted, one of the councillors, Peter Wild (whose brother Richard had been chief justice) moved an amendment that it be declined. Wild's move was seconded but lost and the original motion was passed by a substantial majority.

Blazey was often asked if he was in favour of the tour and he invariably replied that as chairman, he did not have the luxury of a personal view. There was a suspicion — but only a suspicion — that he was not in favour but that he was bound to go along with whatever the council decided. As chairman, he was not required to vote.

That was the tour that was canned two months later because of legal action brought by two rugby club members who contended the tour flouted the union's constitutional obligation to serve the interests of rugby. An interim injunction against the tour was granted in the High Court and the New Zealand union abandoned the tour because it would not have time to contest a substantive hearing.

This led directly to the rebel tour the following year when those All Blacks (with some exceptions) who had already been chosen in 1985 decided to tour anyway, but as 'the Cavaliers'. This tour did go ahead but it brought about a collapse in relations between the New Zealand and South African unions and an end to any sporting contact until 1992, by which time apartheid was in the process of being dismantled.

Blazey recalled how, when he first learned of the rebel tour at a rugby conference in England, he confronted Craven and told him the tour was unacceptable.

Craven, highly qualified academically and perfectly fluent in English, said in his best Afrikaans accent, according to Blazey, 'What does unacceptable mean?'

The rebel All Blacks of 1986 whose tour led to a breakdown of relations between the South African and New Zealand unions.

A Christchurch businessman, Russ Thomas, took over as chairman from Blazey in April of 1986 and it was he who had to guide the NZRFU through the consequences of the rebel tour, though Blazey continued to liaise with the union's lawyers.

The council met on July 10, 1986 to decide what to do about the players who had gone against its wishes. They were declared ineligible for one international match against France on the grounds they did not meet residential requirements and were suspended for one match (against Australia). Even still, it can now be revealed, the council was split. Blazey recalled later that the vote to keep the rebel players out of two tests was by no means unanimous.

The situation in South Africa since the late 1950s and the growing consciousness of the wrong that apartheid wrought split the country, and there was no deeper split than in 1981. The death rattle of those in the mid-1980s who still wanted to play against South Africa split rugby itself.

Champs or Cheats?

For all the praise heaped on the 1905–06 All Blacks, both then and later, there was also condemnation. As the two footballing worlds, the home of the game and its most distant outpost, collided, it was inevitable there would be disagreements about how the game ought to be played.

The New Zealanders introduced what was described as scientific methods to Britain: the players trained regularly and plotted their moves on blackboards rather than, as was the ruling habit in Britain, of just showing up on the day and trusting to natural talent and instinct.

The All Blacks also brought system to the forwards. Instead of the practice in Britain of forwards packing down in order of arrival at scrums, the New Zealanders had designated positions according to body type and practice. The irony of a supposed rural country introducing specialisation into an industrialised country was not lost on those who followed the tour, even though the rural base of rugby in New Zealand was often overstated.

The greatest criticism of the All Blacks, especially in Wales, was of the wing forward, a position that New Zealand had made its own. The wing forward's origins have historically been in dispute — that early innovator of New Zealand rugby, Tom Ellison, has often been credited with inventing the position but there is evidence that it was used in New Zealand long before Ellison's day, at least as early as 1876, and that it had also found favour in the north of England before clubs there went off and formed their own game that later came to be known as rugby league.

Ron Palenski Collection

The Originals' captain, Dave Gallaher.

The wing forward, according to the prevailing view in 1905, was a cheat, pure and simple, and this refrain of outrage continued in British rugby until 1931 when the International Rugby Board eventually outlawed it.

The wing forward was, in essence, an extra halfback. Its existence was owed to the unusual forward formation — unusual to other countries — adopted by New Zealand in scrums: the two-three-two which, according to those who played in it, was the perfect formation. The ball was hooked much more cleanly and quickly in such a scrummaging arrangement and the New Zealand contention was that the wing forward was needed because the halfback could not put the ball in and then get round the back in time to retrieve it.

The most vilified of the New Zealand wing forwards in 1905 was the captain, Dave Gallaher. There is a tale that has often been told that during a game in Wales a woman sitting in the stand kept leaping to her feet, shouting comments such as 'Gallaher, you're a cheat!' Gallaher was bemused by this because he sat that game out and was sitting behind the woman.

The criticism of Gallaher was at two levels: one because of the wing forward position which was seen as being offside; and the other for putting the ball in crooked (Gallaher more often assuming that role than the halfback, Freddy Roberts).

Gallaher had very little to say for himself during the tour, partly because he was evidently a taciturn sort of a chap but mainly because the team on board ship on the way to Britain decided that only manager George Dixon could talk to reporters. During the tour, therefore, Gallaher did not answer his critics. He had his say at the end, however, when he co-operated in the publication of a book, *Why the 'All Blacks' Triumphed*, a compilation of match reports and various comments put together by the rugby writer of the *Daily Mail*, J. A. Buttery.

Gallaher was also co-author of a book with Billy Stead, *The Complete Rugby Footballer*, which was said to have been written by the multi-talented Stead while Gallaher organised photographs and read proofs. The book was supposedly written in a week while the All Blacks were waiting for their ship to New York but evidence is lacking to support such a prodigious feat. Rod Chester and Neville McMillan, in their book marking 100

NZ Rugby Museum

Jim Parker (No. 15) of the Invincibles, shows why the wing forward position was so disliked and criticised. He is plainly preventing a Cornwall player getting through to the All Black halfback, Jimmy Mill.

years of All Black tours, *Centenary*, said Gallaher was contracted by the Harmsworth Magazine Publishing Company to write the book. Yet the book was published by Methuen while the Harmsworth Company was part of the stable that produced the *Daily Mail* and Buttery's book (Alfred Harmsworth, later Lord Northcliffe, founded the *Daily Mail* and the *Daily Mirror* and later owned *The Times* and the *Observer*). The current publisher Methuen is but a fragment and distant descendant of the company that operated under that name in 1905. Its archives, which may have contained evidence of how the Gallaher-Stead book came to be written and over what period, were destroyed by a German bombing raid on London in 1943.

There is no confusion, though, about what Gallaher wrote in Buttery's book. His contribution was multi-headed: 'Secret of our success. "All Black" skipper denies charges of unfair play. Advantages of the wing forward and five-eighths.'

Gallaher wrote:

> The outcry against the wing forward assumed a very bitter tone in south Wales . . . it seemed as if the pent-up indignation of the whole race for years had been let loose on us, and on me particularly. The Welshmen have got a fixed idea in their minds that the wing forward must be offside directly he made a move — no matter how he went or where the ball was.

Gallaher said the wing forward controversy became complicated through the work of ill-informed and irresponsible journalists accusing him of putting bias on the ball when putting it into the scrum.

'The suggestion is ridiculous in the extreme,' he wrote. 'It is impossible to put bias on a football when putting it into a scrum. I defy anyone to do it or show me how it can be done . . . I am sure I could not do it — I have never tried, to tell the truth.'

Gallaher thought there was a great deal of misapprehension about the wing forward and said that if the All Blacks had called him a halfback, there probably would have been no problem.

> But people imagined, because he was new to them, that a wing forward was a terrible person, with a double dose of original football sin. And what amused me throughout this phase of the bother was that nearly all our opponents themselves played wing forwards, although they called them halves.

Gallaher argued that the wing forward was perfectly legitimate providing he kept behind the ball and that, with so many hostile eyes constantly on him, he was careful always to ensure he was. 'But this over-running of the ball happens every day in the case of the ordinary Welsh or English or Irish or Scottish half.' When they got in front of the ball, the crowd saw it as a mistake. When Gallaher did, it was seen as a wilful move.

> I can quite understand how the wing forward seemed an unnecessary sort of excrescence to the home players. The wing forward, as we play it, is the embodiment of an idea, a system of play, which is new here. They stick to the style of the old halfback who puts the ball in the scrum and then runs round and picks it up as it comes out the back. That antique method would be impossible with us. The New Zealand half (or wing forward), after putting the ball in, could not possibly get round to the back of the scrum in time. Our scrum heels out much too quickly for that.

One of the British newspapers critical of the wing forward, the weekly *Winning Post*, indicated the fault with the position could lie with who filled it. 'Tweedledum and Tweedledee' in an open letter to the All Blacks headed 'Teaching Your Grandmother' had this to say:

> We confess that we do not like your wing forward and consider him rather a blot on your game. Moreover, he does not strike us as being in any way

essential, though we admit when your skipper is playing in that position he gets through an enormous amount of work. But his understudies are not nearly as successful as he is, and seem to incur the ban of the referee much more than he does.

In essence, the IRB by outlawing the wing forward 26 years later ensured the perpetuation of what Gallaher described as an antique method — the method that is still in use today. The 1905 All Blacks, and other New Zealand teams, saw the wing forward as an aid to getting the ball out to the backs as quickly as possible and thus ensuring a fast, attacking game. It should be noted too that the accusations that Gallaher put the ball in crooked were to become a familiar refrain on following All Black tours, and most especially against Sid Going in 1972–73.

Scott — Prince of Fullbacks

It is a common problem in rugby, or in any sphere of life if it comes to that, to adequately convey greatness across eras. It is easy to say that Billy Wallace of 1905 fame was one of the greatest players to wear the All Black jersey. It has been said so often it is accepted now without question.

The same can be said of George Nepia and Bert Cooke of the Invincibles and of a few other players. But as time erodes memories and as other players come along, greatness tends to stay captured within the compartments of generations. A player who was a bright and shining star to one generation may barely have been heard of by another.

Compounding the difficulty of comparisons across eras is the way rugby itself has changed, as change it must if it is to remain a 'living' game and not be an anachronistic throwback. The rapidly changing systems of aiding memories also have an effect. It is a simple process to watch a DVD or a tape, for example, of All Blacks of the 1980s or 90s and again see them in action, again appreciate what they did in the time in which they had to do it. It is less easy to see players of earlier eras; impossible to see some.

There are names which transcend these difficulties. Wallace, Nepia and Cooke are examples. Another is Robert William Henry Scott, known to a generation or more as Bob Scott, fullback for the ages.

He was once asked, amid a range of questions about the time in his life that stamped itself forever in the memories, what it felt like to be dropped from the All Blacks. He did not know, he replied, he never was.

Not only was Scott never dropped, he must be the only All Black to have been twice asked to come out of retirement. Twice? The first is reasonably well known for those who followed his career specifically or for those who have kept a close eye on the highways and byways of All Blacks as they have travelled down the years.

The first time was in 1952. Scott, to recap briefly on a career that should never be dismissed with brevity, first made his name nationally with the army team, the 2nd New Zealand Expeditionary Force Kiwis — the 'Khaki All Blacks'— who toured Europe immediately after the Second World War and who then came home to show how rugby post-war could be played. From then until 1950, Scott was the All Blacks' fullback, as automatic a selection as could ever have been made.

In an era when New Zealand struggled with the balance between forward dominance and back play, between winning rugby and entertaining rugby, Scott was a phenomenon. He did what fullbacks before him had never done and what many since have not been able to do.

Ironically, he considered he played his finest rugby when few New Zealanders could see him — in South Africa in 1949 when all four tests were lost. It was a depressing time for All Black rugby and for Scott personally because he was the goal-kicker and in such a tight series, every kick was crucial. Scott gained some consolation the following year with the winning series against the British Isles.

He 'retired' in 1951 at the age of 30, trailing his clouds of glory. His 'last' first-class match was for Auckland against Hawke's Bay at Eden Park on October 6, 1951. More than a hundred telegrams of best wishes sat by Scott's place in the dressing room, alongside an illuminated address, a brand-new Auckland jersey and a bound volume of that season's programmes, all given to him by a grateful Auckland union. One telegram among the many that Scott may have prized most was brief and to the point: 'Good luck and God bless you. George Nepia.'

Another tribute, which probably embarrassed Scott, was written by

Ron Palenski Collection

Bob Scott, who still deserves to rank with the greatest of All Black fullbacks.

the sports editor of the Auckland *8 O'Clock*, Esmond Doherty: 'His spirit of adventure on attack, resourcefulness on defence and the sheer artistry of other aspects of his play have gone a long way towards revolutionising previously recognised ideas of fullback play.'

The spirit, resourcefulness and artistry were not long on the shelf. Scott returned to the field the following year to play for the Barbarians at Waikaraka Park in Onehunga against a team designated Auckland Clubs, which was in effect a shadow Auckland representative team.

Scott, according to Doherty, was the outstanding player on the field and, within a fortnight, he was back in the Auckland team. He was still unavailable for international play, or so he thought.

Towards the end of the 1952 season, Scott went to Wellington to play for the Centurions club against Wellington. The big British tour of 1953–54 was still a year away but already it loomed large on the rugby horizon. Rugby minds were already being exercised about which players would best represent New Zealand on just the fourth foray to Britain.

While in Wellington, Scott was approached by what later were described as 'senior rugby men'. Neither he nor his biographer, Terry McLean, would say then or later who the men were. Even years later, when writer Bob Howitt included Scott in his first volume of *Rugby Greats*, the identity remained a mystery. 'Scott still refuses to divulge their names,' Howitt wrote.

The buttonholing of the reluctant Scott took place at the Midland Hotel on Lambton Quay, one of the three Wellington hotels (the others were the Grand and the St George) that served as hostelry and unofficial headquarters of New Zealand rugby. And the buttonholer was Clarrie Gibbons, then a Wellington selector and a man well-known in sporting circles throughout New Zealand. He was an emissary, Scott now says, for Tom Morrison, a former All Black and one of the men charged with selecting the team for Britain.

Scott recorded in his biography written with McLean that he was astounded and jolted by the request for him to make himself available for the British tour. They were perfectly adequate words for the 1950s. 'I was blown away' is likely to be a modern equivalent.

A week after this and while Scott was mulling over the unexpected request, he and George Nepia were on the same rugby field at the same time. Scott was a player, this time for the Olympians club against Poverty Bay in Gisborne, and Nepia was the referee. Towards the end of the game, a little rugby history was made. Fred Allen, well into the twilight of his playing days, scored a try to take the Olympians out to 34–14. Allen tossed the ball to Scott for the conversion but Scott, in a gesture that delighted the crowd, tossed it to Nepia. From one famous All Black fullback to another. Nepia rolled back the years and kicked the conversion, then resumed his refereeing duties.

Scott kept his counsel for the rest of 1952 and said publicly early in 1953 that he was coming out of retirement and would be available for national selection. His comments drew some criticism because it was assumed that Scott figured he only had to lace up his boots to be chosen. That may have been the case, in fact probably was the case, but Scott, a modest and self-effacing man, would never have thought that. 'All I did was make myself available like hundreds of other players,' he said. 'I still had to play well enough to be chosen.'

The rest is history. He was, of course, chosen. He went to Britain with the All Blacks and was lauded wherever he and the team went.

If Doctor Who can be indulged and modern rugby be transported back to the early 1950s, Scott would be the most familiar face in the country. He would be in television commercials, he would be on billboards, he would be the face of All Black rugby. He would be a multi-millionaire.

Scott returned to New Zealand from an All Black tour which, like its immediate predecessor in 1935–36 and every one since, bore the burden of trying to match the feats of 1905 and 1924, however unrealistic that may have been. Scott returned, this time, to retirement.

What is not widely known was that Scott was asked again to come out of retirement in the national cause. Two years later, in 1956, New Zealand

Generations of greatness: Don Clarke, Bob Scott, George Nepia and Billy Wallace at Athletic Park in 1967.

was in an intense state — at least rugby was — about the pending visit of the South Africans for the series that ranks still among the most gripping played. New Zealand rugby was obsessed with exorcising the Springbok ghosts of 1937 and 1949.

The chairman of selectors and coach of the All Blacks was Tom Morrison, at whose request Scott was persuaded out of retirement in 1952. Morrison and his fellow selectors, Arthur Marslin (who had coached the 1953–54 team) and Jack Sullivan (who once captained Scott in a primary school team), were under a pressure the like of which few other national selectors before or since have known. With them as an unofficial selector and coach of the forwards was Bob Stuart, who had been Scott's captain in 1943–54.

They scoured the country for the best equipped players to beat the

South Africans for the first time in a series. They persuaded one of Scott's contemporaries, prop Kevin Skinner, out of retirement, such was their need for men who would not buckle under the South African pressure. And they tried to persuade Scott. This time, one of the grand old men of rugby, Stan Dean, was the emissary. Dean had managed the Invincibles of 1924–25 and been chairman of the New Zealand union for 25 years until 1947.

'I was very flattered,' Scott recalled recently, 'but I was 35 years old and I hadn't played any serious rugby since 1954. It's hard to say no when your country calls you but I'm afraid I had to.'

Without Scott, the selectors turned to a makeshift fullback, Pat Walsh, for the first two tests (a win and a loss) then introduced Don Clarke for the third and fourth (two wins). With Clarke's debut, the fullback's torch had been passed.

Just how good was Scott? Has the passing of the years heightened perceptions, is his reputation firmly in the grip of the warm glow of nostalgia? For a subjective answer, it is possible to turn to a contemporary, Wilfred Wooller, a Welshman who knew a thing or two about sport. He played rugby for Wales, he captained Glamorgan at cricket and was an England cricket selector. Wooller played against the 1935–36 All Blacks and saw the 1953–54 team from the press boxes. Wooller wrote:

> The outstanding playing personality of both tours I give, without hesitation, to Bob Scott. For sheer attacking artistry from a position usually reserved for defensive security, I have never seen his equal. His positional timing was perfection in person. He typified all the qualities that thrill a rugby follower. He never seemed hurried, seldom failed to elude a charging forward, rarely missed a long screw kick to touch. His drop kick was long and effortless. . . . He will rank with the greatest players of any era.

Or Dai Gent, England halfback against the 1905 All Blacks, a man who had seen Wallace and Nepia at the heights of their glories: 'As a fielder of the ball, kicker of it in every way — punt, drop and place; genius in taking up his position, supporter of the backs and sidestepper against coming up opponents, he is the best I have ever seen.'

Larry Montague, son of the celebrated First World War era journalist and novelist Charles Montague, wrote for the *Guardian*, or the *Manchester Guardian* as it then was. Scott was, he wrote after the All Blacks beat Scotland, incomparable and his play was beyond criticism.

Clem Thomas, another former Welsh player who took to journalism (and an opponent of Scott's) called him the greatest fullback he had seen. Scott and Thomas, incidentally, were the subject of a bit of sensationalist reporting after the All Blacks drew with Swansea. Such was the ill feeling in the match, an unnamed reporter wrote, that Scott and Thomas refused to shake hands. McLean, who covered the tour for the New Zealand Press Association, wrote at the time that the report was wrong and that, in fact, Scott and Thomas were on the best of terms both after that match and after the Welsh test. The reporter was of the view that the 1953–54 All Blacks were not a happy team but McLean, who sometimes was not slow to report on the inner feelings of an All Black camp, denied it.

'As one who has the privilege of travelling and living in intimate daily association with the All Blacks, I would unhesitatingly describe them as a singularly happy party,' he wrote.

There was the occasional problem, though, and Scott stepped in to fix it. McLean wrote in Scott's book that some of the players took to mimicking the way the manager, Norman Millard, spoke, in particular a habit of emphasising words mid-sentence. An England selector approached McLean and told him the players were making fun of the manager. McLean got hold of Scott, who had been elected — by one vote over Kevin Skinner — as the players' representative on the tour selection committee. McLean told Scott he would do something about it.

'No you won't,' McLean quoted Scott as replying, 'it's got nothing to do with you. You leave this to me.'

McLean wrote that a puerile piece of humour within the team and a gross breach of manners outside it ceased completely.

It was an illustration, small as it may have been, of the standing and respect Scott had among his team-mates. He was respected not just as a player but for the way in which he behaved off the field as well as on it.

He also had — has — a nice droll sense of humour or, as McLean once put it, 'a bit of the imp in him'.

McLean wrote about the All Blacks being in the Scottish Borders and some of the players went to Abbotsford, the home of Sir Walter Scott, and a nearby statue of Scott.

Scott reached up to one of the stone hands and said gravely, 'How are you, Uncle?' One great Scott to another.

Beware the 'P' Word

The All Black hooker, Anton Oliver, was a little bemused when he was criticised for reaching for a wartime analogy amid the devastation of the World Cup quarter-final loss to France in 2007.

Soon after the end of the match, when a nation's hopes died and were buried at the Millennium Stadium, Oliver said characteristically that he had recently been reading two books, *Massacre at Passchendaele*, an account of New Zealand's role in the horrific 1917 First World War battle, and the German novel about life in the trenches in the same war, *All Quiet on the Western Front*.

'The feeling in the shed was like no-man's-land, as it's described in those two books,' Oliver said. 'Desolate. Decay. The smell of death. That's what it feels like for us. It's not a nice place to be.'

New Zealand on October 6, 2007 lost a rugby match that it probably should have won. New Zealand on October 12, 1917 lost a battle it could never have won. More than 1100 New Zealanders were killed, the biggest daily death toll in the country's history.

Oliver, who likes to learn about the past and take lessons from it, never meant to offend or to belittle the extent of the disaster of 1917; neither did he mean to overstate the significance of a sporting loss in 2007. He wasn't equating one with the other; merely trying to say that the mood in the dressing room, the feeling of empty despair, was evocative to him of what he read about no-man's-land, the space of desolation between war's frontlines.

But he was castigated for the comment as New Zealanders reached out, perhaps not as blindly as in 1999 after a similar loss, to vent their feelings about once more having to face the fact the team they were constantly told was the best in the world could not win the tournament that would anoint them with that title.

Oliver's comments were a particularly inflammable fuel for those people who ring radio stations.

Perhaps the trigger word in Oliver's comments was Passchendaele. Few New Zealanders would know much about the detail of the battle that was formally known as the Third Battle of Ypres, but all surely would be aware of the emotive connotations of the word. All would know that something dreadful happened there.

Oliver was not the first senior All Black figure to tumble into trouble because of the use of the P-word.

Ivan Vodanovich, an All Black prop who coached New Zealand in South Africa in 1970 and against the British Isles in 1971, also once let the word slip and realised later he would have spared himself had he chosen another word. Vodanovich, like Oliver, did not intend to offend and was in all respects a mild-mannered man with a nicely developed sense of humour and an even keener sense of duty to New Zealand rugby.

But he had not liked what he saw when the Lions played Canterbury on the Saturday before the first test. One newspaper called the game, won by the Lions 14–3, 'a blot on rugby and on the good sportsmanship of New Zealanders'. It was called torrid, fiery, violent and vicious.

Three of the Lions, props Sandy Carmichael and Ray McLoughlin, and flanker Mike Hipwell, were taken to hospital. For Carmichael, with a broken eye socket and McLoughlin with a broken thumb, the tour was over.

Even Larry Saunders in the Christchurch *Star Sports*, normally fiercely parochial and supportive of Canterbury rugby, had this to say:

There was some really rough, tough stuff in the tight exchanges with players scragging each other with determination and even venom.

Some of the Canterbury players were far from blameless in these hectic goings-on, but the Lions certainly did not hesitate to meet them halfway in these abrasive differences.

The other main Christchurch rugby writer at the time, John Brooks, wrote in the *Press* that a seam of sourness ran through the game. He summed up the root of the problem:

The trouble could have been nipped in the bud in the early stages. M. L. Hipwell, a Lions flanker, displayed a penchant for getting into the Canterbury side of the rucks and A. J. Wyllie was uncompromising in his efforts to remove him. The Lions were penalised 11 times but not once for a ruck infringement.

At the after-match function, Lions captain John Dawes remarked he was pleased that the referee, Humphrey Rainey from Wellington, was a doctor.

The more telling comment after the match was made by Vodanovich to Bob Howitt, who then wrote rugby for the *Sunday News*. He accused the Lions of nullifying the possibility of second-phase play by lying on the ball in rucks and making no attempt to get free. It was doing this that caused their injuries.

'The same thing will happen in the first test if the All Blacks cannot get at the ball,' he told Howitt. 'If the Lions persist with these tactics, Carisbrook could become another Passchendaele.'

It needs to be understood that in 1971, there were still a great many First World War veterans in New Zealand and families with sorrowful knowledge of what had happened at Passchendaele. There were also many men in positions of rugby authority who had served in the Second World War who knew at first-hand the terrors and costs of war and knew all too well the import of the word 'Passchendaele'.

Terry McLean, who covered the tour for the *New Zealand Herald*, himself a war veteran, said he was outraged by the comment and told Vodanovich so when he ran into him at Wellington airport the next day.

McLean asked the chairman of the New Zealand union, Jack Sullivan, what he thought of the All Black coach making such a comment and Sullivan, who was severely wounded in the Second World War in fighting near Tobruk, replied the use of the word 'battle' was inappropriate. Sullivan would not utter the word Passchendaele.

Curiously, neither did McLean when he reported the comments to *The Times* in London. He wrote that Vodanovich had warned Carisbrook 'could become a battlefield'.

The chairman of the New Zealand Rugby Referees Association, 'Brit' Matthews, was also chairman of the Horowhenua County Council, and was at a meeting of local body officials in Wellington when talk turned to the rugby events of the weekend. He said he and his colleagues were appalled by Vodanovich's comments and agreed he should be told to resign. 'I was extremely disturbed,' he said.

Ron Palenski Collection

All Black coach Ivan Vodanovich and his test captain, Colin Meads, in a pre-match chat before the third test against the Lions in 1971.

One provincial rugby union, Poverty Bay, also called for Vodanovich to be replaced.

Both the Lions manager, Doug Smith, and the coach, Carwyn James, reacted publicly with dismay and privately with fury to Vodanovich's comments — both the use of the word Passchendaele and his accusations about the Lions lying on the ball.

James, an expert in Welsh history and language as well as rugby, said Passchendaele was as evocative a word in Wales as it was in New Zealand and he was saddened that it was used in the context of a rugby match. 'It was too emotive a term to use — to all of us it is very unfortunate.'

The British press latched on to the story with gusto. The *Daily Mail* headed its story 'It's rugby war' and the *Daily Mirror* followed suit with 'Rugby's total war'. Their comments were directed more at the mood of the match itself rather than in Vodanovich's reaction, although David Frost in the *Guardian* said Vodanovich's comments were inflammatory.

New Zealand lost face and friends with the manner of Canterbury's play, Frost wrote. 'In the first place Canterbury descended to the lowest level of thuggery from the very start, hitting the Lions with fists, knees or boots at set scrums and lineouts and even in the open field,' he wrote. 'It was brutal and utterly out of character with the rest of the tour. Canterbury should be struck off the itinerary of the next Lions tour of New Zealand.'

The Times said the match atmosphere 'became unspeakable when the open terrace spectators, who numbered most of the 53,000 present, howled for the blood of "the Poms"'.

Canterbury was the war before the peace, as it turned out. The first test was hard and competitive, as any test should be, but contained none of the violence that had marked the game the week before. The All Blacks, like Canterbury, dominated possession and territory but, like Canterbury, also lost.

The last word was left with McLean who felt no compunction about choosing another battle name (though not one in which New Zealanders were involved): rather than Passchendaele, he wrote, the first test was the All Blacks' Waterloo.

A Rivalry for the Ages

There's no surer sign of the infrequency of victory than the frequency of its commemoration. If victory is commonplace, it is accepted as unremarkable and merely an indication of the accepted order of things. But a rare victory. That is entirely different.

Every All Black who has been in Wales, and every New Zealand supporter who has followed tours in Wales, will have seen, heard or read of how victories against the All Blacks are reverently remembered. Those who actually saw such victories, much less those who contributed to them, are now among diminishing numbers. But what does not diminish is the fact: for more than half a century, the All Blacks were under threat in Wales more than anywhere else. From 1905 until 1972, All Black teams lost just seven times in the British Isles and six of those losses were in Wales.

Just to emphasise the point, when the Welsh Rugby Union did New Zealand the honour of inviting the All Blacks as their centenary year showpiece in 1980, the itinerary incorporated each of the teams which could claim New Zealand on their roll of honour — Cardiff, Swansea, Llanelli, Newport and Wales.

New Zealanders now might wonder what all the excitement was about. No one under the age of 50 has lived through an All Black loss to a Welsh team. When the All Blacks last lost to Wales, Winston Churchill was the British prime minister; trams still plied the streets of New Zealand cities; Ed Hillary was still being described in newspaper stories as a beekeeper; New Zealand passports still bore the identifier, 'British subject'.

An early example of the rugby photographer's art: New Zealand and Wales in 1905.

Even during their golden era of the 1970s, Wales could not beat the All Blacks, although they went desperately close. Only occasionally since has Wales been able to rattle the All Black cage of superiority, even on occasion being beaten by scores that are more associated with the lesser teams of world rugby.

But any New Zealander who was in Cardiff for the World Cup quarter-final in 2007, or any other time when the All Blacks have played there, could not fail to pick up the intensity of feeling that remains for rugby. The Welsh may now play, as one of their great players, Gerald Davies, once wrote, with one eye looking back on their past, but there is no mistaking that rugby is still a vitally significant part of being Welsh.

On test day in central Cardiff, the pubs are full and the streets are thronged. The scarlet jerseys of Wales, the dragon flag, giant leeks, and what Dylan Thomas called the 'fine, live people, the spirit of Wales itself', are everywhere.

History is at every turn. The Angel Hotel of many rugby memories, some of them unhappy for New Zealanders, is across the road from the Millennium Stadium which, of course, is plonked on the site that once was

A small section of the crowd that crammed the Arms Park for the All Blacks' first test against Wales.

Cardiff Arms Park. Along the road in a shopping mall is a statue of the great Welsh halfback, Gareth Edwards. Also across the road from the stadium is a restaurant that was once owned (and maybe still is) by Barry John, another revered figure of the golden era (but another, like Edwards, whose success against New Zealand was in the scarlet of the Lions and not of Wales).

There once was a time that both teams stayed in the central city hotels, all within a brief walk of the stadium. The lobbies of their hotels were packed with people looking for tickets, or just looking. When it came time to go to the ground, players walked through the crowds, backs slapped, best wishes shouted. No one then talked about players 'connecting' with their fans; there was no need. These days, teams stay in seclusion in country clubs or five-star hotels out of the city and drive into the stadium in tour buses, the figures of fame just a blur behind tinted glass. The supporters miss out and maybe the players do too.

Some players have not liked being in Wales, have been repelled by the intensity of feeling, the clash of nationalisms at close quarters; the repetitious cries of 'wait till you get to Wales' throughout the United Kingdom, the cries of 'Wales will beat you' once there.

But some players thrive on it, others simply respect it as being a part of rugby, a part of touring, much like in New Zealand. One All Black, Brad Johnstone, refused to return to Wales. But one of his team-mates, Bryan Williams, could hardly have anything but fond thoughts for the place. How could he not when he stood alone in the goldfish bowl of the Arms Park and the crowd of 50,000 sang for him, just for him?

We'll keep a welcome in the hillsides,
We'll keep a welcome in the vales.
This land you know will still be singing,
When you come home again to Wales.

Maybe crowds in Wales don't sing now like they used to, maybe younger generations of Welsh people don't have the nonconformist fervour of earlier times, maybe the plastic society and the all-pervasive American influence has wiped out some of the distinctive Welshness, but the crowds still sing 'Cwm Rhondda' with its wonderfully apposite line: *'When I tread the verge of Jordan; Bid my anxious fears subside. . .'*

The touchlines are the players' verge of Jordan; no player could tread them without wishing away their anxious fears. Where the players of today have trod, so too all the players before them.

For New Zealand, it all began on December 16, 1905, and few New Zealanders or Welsh at any time in the more than hundred years since should need telling what happened on that day. On a wall in the New Zealand Sports Hall of Fame in Dunedin some old scoreboard signs carry the message: Wales 3, New Zealand 0. No matter that the original scoreboard in Cardiff read 'Seland Newydd'. Welsh visitors delight in its presence; they take photos of it, they tell others of it.

But as is often the case in rugby, it wasn't so much the score but how it was arrived at. The most enduring of New Zealand rugby writers (his rugby writing life began in 1930 and his last tour was 1987), Terry McLean, once wrote of the 1905 test against Wales as 'the greatest match of all'. Some of his travelling companions often teased him about 1905 and asked him where he sat among the crowd of 40,000 and whether he got a decent view of when Bob Deans said he scored and when the referee, John Dallas, said he did not.

No rugby test could have been written and spoken about as much as that match on a grey afternoon in Cardiff. A hundred years later, it was the subject of a book — called, inevitably, *The Greatest Game Ever Played*, and 101 years later it was the subject of acrimony between the All Blacks and the Welsh Rugby Union (when the All Blacks did their haka in the dressing room).

It is remembered, talked about, argued about, mostly but not wholly because it was the All Blacks' only loss on their first tour of Britain and because Deans thought he had scored and thus could have — not necessarily would have — preserved the All Blacks' unbeaten record. There have been innumerable other incidents when one side or another has been denied a score that would have determined the outcome of a match but none has prompted even a tiny fraction of the comment the way 1905 has.

It was the first time the All Blacks played Wales and that was significant in itself. The All Blacks went to Britain determined to show 'the Mother Country' how well the far-flung colony had adapted to the game that came from England's public schools. Wales was the strength of British rugby at the time and how the All Blacks fared there would be the barometer of the tour.

The match also gave rise to the enduring ritual of rugby test matches, the haka and the singing of national anthems. The Welsh Rugby Union had sent people to some of the New Zealand games in England and they reported not just on aspects of play, but on the fact that the All Blacks preceded some matches (but not all) with a 'war dance'. Among the tactics devised by the Welsh therefore was a counter to the haka. 'Land of My Fathers' had been written in 1856 and had the description if not the status of national anthem in 1905. The Welsh union agreed with a suggestion that their players should sing it after the haka and when they did, when the opening bars of 'Mae hen wlad fy nhadau yn annwyl i mi . . .' drifted across to the crowd, thousands joined in. It was affirmation of an anthem.

The match was significant in itself; the fact Wales won made it even more so. The All Blacks, according to the Welsh Rugby Union official historians, contributed enormously to the future of the sport in Wales. Some of the All Blacks, they said, would be haunted to the end by the Welsh days of the tour.

The Deans 'try' became central to the standing the match acquired in rugby lore because it injected some mystery, an unprovable factor, into a sporting encounter that was already charged with significance. The incident, wrote historians David Smith and Gareth Williams, was 'the grit in the oyster that produced a black pearl for later generations'.

It is a part of New Zealand rugby knowledge that Deans, after a break by Billy Wallace, forced the ball over the line for what seemed a legitimate try only for him to be pulled back into the field of play. The referee, John Dallas, was dressed in ordinary street clothes, as the story goes, and arrived too late on the scene to know what had happened and ruled no try.

It has been argued about ever since, first by the participants and later by those who said they saw it or had been told by participants, later still by people who once spoke to someone who spoke to someone else who heard something from someone else. By such processes does oral history survive.

Seldom does the poor old referee, John Dallas, get a look in, at least in New Zealand accounts.

It is not seldom acknowledged that he was a fit young man, well capable of keeping up with play. The impression given in the most often told tales in New Zealand was that Dallas was some old fogey of a referee who panted along in the far distance and could not keep up with the players. In fact,

Dallas at the time was 27 years old and just over 18 months before had played for Scotland against England. He was therefore in the same age bracket as the players (and younger than both captains) and must have been intimately familiar with the modern game as it was then. Yes, he wore what could be described as street clothes but so did every other referee of the time, as photos amply demonstrate.

Bob Deans himself and various other New Zealanders have frequently been quoted, then and later, about their version of events; similarly various Welshmen have had their say and the one given most publicity in New Zealand was Teddy Morgan, the scorer of Wales's try, who wrote on a dinner menu when the All Blacks were again in Wales in 1924 that Deans did score.

Dallas is less often quoted, yet he wrote a letter within days of the match. He arrived home in Edinburgh and said he was astonished to read on the Monday morning that Deans had 'scored' a try that he had disallowed.

Dallas then explained his view:

> When the ball went back on its way out to Deans I kept going hard and when Deans was tackled he grounded the ball six to twelve inches short of the goal-line. At that moment he could neither pass nor play the ball and as I passed between the Welsh goalposts my whistle went shrill and loud. It is true that when I got to the spot to order a scrum the ball was over the goal-line, but without hesitation I ordered a scrum at the place where Deans was grounded. I never blew my whistle at the spot. It had gone before. No try was scored by Deans.

The fact Dallas was a Scot was not lost on the New Zealanders. They did not have warm feelings toward Scotland because of the way they had been treated there. The *Guardian*, a few days after the Welsh match, quoted an unidentified member of the New Zealand party as saying he was 'certain that any native of Scotland necessarily, by previous events, be forced into prejudice against New Zealand events'.

The version most liked in New Zealand came from the telegram Deans sent to the *Daily Mail* in London on the Sunday morning after the match: 'Grounded ball 6 inches over line some of Welsh players admit try Hunter and Glasgow can confirm was pulled back by Welshmen before referee arrived Deans.'

Clarity over what did or did not happen was not helped by the fact that various players were named as responsible for tackling Deans and then hauling him back, and some accounts also attributed the 'try' to one or other of the New Zealanders. The All Black manager, George Dixon, asserted a try had been scored and credence was given to his comments because he was listed in the programme as one of the touch judges (though wrongly listed as president of the New Zealand union) and therefore closer to the action than any in the crowd. Some reports, though, said that the All Blacks' vice-captain, Billy Stead, was the New Zealand touch judge and still others said George Nicholson was. (It was common practice then for the two teams to provide the touch judges.)

Stead made no mention in his newspaper columns for the *Southland Times* of being touch judge but he recorded rather matter of factly that each team scored a try but that Dallas would not allow New Zealand's. Dallas was, according to Stead, a referee 'picked against our express wish and protest'.

Deans died just over two years later and there is a story — unprovable as are so many about this match — that even on his deathbed, he swore that he had scored against Wales. This was picked up by the Welshman said to have tackled him, Rhys Gabe.

'So much importance has been attached to the utterance of Bob Deans on his deathbed,' Gabe wrote. 'I can say, when I shall be in the same condition, that I who tackled him was positive he did not score.'

The supposed deathbed comment was put to Dallas by the manager of the 1935 All Blacks in Britain, Vin Meredith. 'If he did say that,' Meredith quoted Dallas as saying, 'then he went to meet his Maker with a lie on his lips.'

Of course, if such an incident occurred today or at any time in the past 30 years it would be captured by television cameras and be subject to endless replays in slow motion and with any number of talking heads offering their opinions. But then there would be no mystery and rugby would be the poorer.

Stead hints at the real reason why the All Blacks lost. It had nothing to do with whether Deans did or did not score. The All Black backs had a shocker of a game, as Stead candidly conceded. For a start, New Zealand were without three crucial players, forward Bill Cunningham and backs Stead and George Smith (although Stead did not mention himself).

New Zealand attempts to find the line, give or take passes or even to field a ball were absolutely painful to watch, Stead wrote. 'Never on this tour has our back play fallen to so low a standard and it was quite evident to us who know the men that they must have been prey to . . . nervous excitement.' The Welsh, however, rose to the occasion 'and playing as never a Welsh team ever played (I have the authority of old internationals in saying this) they got the score in and kept it as close as possible'.

They got the score. Nothing else mattered.

Guns 'n Pumas

By any standards, the All Blacks' tour of Argentina in 1976 was unusual —even bizarre at times and downright dangerous, or at least frightening, at others. It was a tour that would never be contemplated today but if it were, as improbable as that is, there would be howls of protest.

The anguish would come from different sources for different reasons. The tour completed a year in which 56 different All Blacks were chosen, reason enough for outrage by those who see the jersey as being devalued. The players would have their complaints too. For a few days in 1976 when the All Blacks were in Uruguay, they did not receive the daily allowance to which amateur players were then entitled. How players today would react to not being paid has not yet been tested.

Argentina was a volatile country in 1976 and several players at different times were confronted by people wielding guns. The reaction to such an occurrence on an All Black tour now can be imagined: there'd be no end of meetings with lawyers, agents, security advisers, psychologists and consultants.

But the outrage would not have been just within rugby. Argentina in 1976 was a martial state. It is well documented that human rights were routinely abused or ignored by the military government and its agents. A different lot of All Blacks earlier that year had been to South Africa, much to the annoyance of a good many New Zealanders and much of what is euphemistically known as the international community. The opposition to South Africa was caused by its apartheid policy which bestowed full rights on white people and very few on anyone else. The irony that the 'second' All Blacks went to a country where rights were just as subjectively dispensed with but there was not a peep from protesters anywhere was not lost on the players.

Another factor that was rare then and impossible today when television has such a grip on the game was that the tour was not carried out in the full glare of the modern publicity machine. Only two New Zealand newspaper reporters accompanied the All Blacks; there was no regular radio coverage (although the BBC's man in Buenos Aires did his best) and no television. The All Black captain, Graham Mourie, aptly borrowed a couple of lines from Thomas Gray's 'Elegy Written in a Country Churchyard' for an epigraph to begin the chapter in his book about Argentina:

Full many a flower is born to blush unseen,
And waste its sweetness on the desert air.

Mourie himself was one of the flowers whose sweetness was not wasted; he was introduced to the test side the following year for two of the tests against the Lions and, by the end of 1977, had succeeded Tane Norton as the All Black captain. Stu Wilson was another. He was regarded then more as a centre than as a wing, and Argentina proved to be the stepping stone for him to full All Black status and ultimately a secure place in the history of the game. Andy Haden was another. He had been a callow All Black in 1972–73 in Britain, shown his original way of thinking by becoming among the first to ply his trade as a rugby player (once even playing in both England and Italy for different clubs on the same weekend), and probably should have gone to South Africa in 1976. The Argentine marked his resurrection as an All Black. He was a towering influence for good on the team both on and off the field and his high status was never again questioned.

The tour was also the metamorphosis of the coach, Jack Gleeson. A 49-year-old publican from Feilding, Gleeson had played for Manawatu as a wing in the early 1950s and was a selector for the province for much of the 1960s.

He became a New Zealand selector in 1972 and was immediately given the onerous task of being both manager and coach of the All Blacks on an internal tour in 1972; aside from the dual role, he was also on a hiding to nothing. Anything less than dominant wins against provincial opposition would have been the end of Gleeson. He got the dominant wins, but not the rewards. He was consigned back to the national Under 21 team until the NZRU entrusted him with the All Blacks, albeit a second choice team, for Argentina.

He was a revelation. Quietly spoken and thoughtful and with an enormous respect for the silver fern, he turned a group of disparate players who weren't quite sure of their status into a team of winners. 'Play the game at pace and be a thinker,' was his dictum and that's what the All Blacks did against a Pumas team that was then emerging onto the world scene. The All Blacks arrived in Argentina in time to see the Pumas on television in Cardiff all but beating Wales, who were then close to the height of their powers.

Before Argentina, Gleeson's future was uncertain. After Argentina, it was guaranteed. He took over the All Blacks against the Lions in 1977, then in France later that year, against Australia in 1978 and then his crowning achievement, coaching the All Blacks to their first grand slam in Britain. It was on the grand slam tour that Gleeson let it be known quietly to a few people close to him that he was not feeling all that well. Cancer claimed him within a year.

Gleeson's great advocate on the New Zealand union council was Ron Don, the Aucklander who was most commonly described as 'feisty' or 'peppery'. That was largely because he was the most identifiable and vocal supporter of continued rugby with South Africa among national administrators. He made no bones about it. The All Blacks should play South Africa, end of story, was the nub of his argument. Any other considerations were the fault of the news media.

There could be no argument that Don was a committed enthusiast for rugby. He'd been on the Auckland union since 1953 and chairman since 1969. He wanted to be the manager of the All Blacks in Britain in 1972–73,

NZ Rugby Museum

The little-known All Blacks: the team that went to Argentina in 1976.

but was beaten in a ballot by Ernie Todd. He wanted to manage them in Ireland in 1974 but was beaten by Noel Stanley. His ultimate prize would have been managing the All Blacks in South Africa, but that also went to Stanley. Don then stood to become manager in Argentina. The only other candidate was Peter Wild, a Nelsonian who had moved to Auckland and who in 1973 had managed the Junior All Blacks who beat the All Blacks in Dunedin. Don won the ballot.

After he was elected, Don conceded that the tour would be a challenge. It was a common enough response by newly elected managers for any tour. In this case, it was a master of understatement.

It was a challenge even before they left because there was criticism, at least in newspapers, of the players being given the status of All Blacks. Initially, the secretary of the New Zealand union, Jack Jeffs, said the official name would be 'New Zealand XV' but then the chairman, Ces Blazey, went further and said they were an official New Zealand representative team. He added that 'All Blacks' was merely a news media nickname and had no status within the NZRU, a situation that would change within a decade as the money-pulling power of the name dawned on the administrators.

There were also questions about the status of the two matches against Argentina. They would not be official tests, Blazey said, because that status could be given only to matches between member countries of the International Rugby Board. He was questioned about matches in 1949 between a second-string New Zealand team and Australia being official tests and he said that was all right because Australia was an IRB member. He was not asked about All Black tests against France being given full test status even though France was not a member of the IRB until 1978. Logic and consistency were never strong suits in international rugby politics.

No one in New Zealand knew much about Argentine rugby; not much about Argentina either. The Hamilton Marist and Auckland Suburbs clubs had both toured there and Don and Gleeson quizzed them about what to expect but they did not go with the dossiers of information that teams these days see as essential. They learnt some things they may have preferred not to learn. The Hamilton Marist players told them they drank a Buenos Aires rugby club dry in one afternoon, spurred on by Argentina's inflation rate making bottles of beer about 10 cents each.

The All Blacks' tour had three essential elements: the rugby; organisation and logistics which to orderly New Zealand minds were chaotic; and the politics or, at least, the effect of the politics.

The tour began not in Buenos Aires but in the Uruguayan capital, Montevideo, a short flight across the wide expanse of the mouth of the Rio del Plata or, as the English-speaking world knows it, the River Plate. The 1976 All Blacks did not realise it, but All Blacks had been there before. The 1905 team called in at Montevideo on the way to Britain and the players were not impressed. The vice-captain, Billy Stead, wrote his impressions: 'We were immediately besieged by the most motley, heterogeneous crowd it has ever been my misfortune to set my eyes on. The architecture and the stench of the place are its principal features.'

Things had improved since then. The architecture was still grand and ornate, but there was no discernible stench different from any other big city. Neither would the All Blacks have described the Uruguayan people as motley — the impression gained later by comparison was that they were similar in most respects to Argentines: the men handsomely and volubly Latin, the women stylish. More than one player asked rhetorically where the unstylish women were hidden, or words to that effect anyway.

New Zealanders can seldom travel far without some reminder of home, even in the most remote or exotic of locations. The All Blacks were met at the airport by an ageing expatriate waving a New Zealand flag. He was, he said, the only New Zealander in Uruguay and had been there farming for 30 or so years. He became a tour regular. Outside the team's hotel, hawkers sold the normal range of tourist postcards but among them were black and white images of scenes from the aftermath of the Battle of the River Plate, the first major naval battle of the Second World War. Montevideo was where the German pocket battleship, the *Admiral Graf Spee*, sought refuge after being attacked by the three British ships, the *Ajax*, the *Exeter* and the New Zealand-manned *Achilles*. One of the postcards showed the *Graf Spee* burning after it was scuttled in the River Plate off Montevideo.

The All Blacks may not have known much about a naval battle of 37 years before but they did know of Uruguay's main claim to rugby fame: the story of the players who survived an air crash in the high Andes warding off starvation by eating the flesh of their dead team-mates. Two of the survivors were at a dinner for both teams after the New Zealand–Uruguay game. There were a few macabre asides, uttered sotto voce, from the All Blacks.

Just how different Latin American rugby was to what the All Blacks were used to was amply demonstrated in Montevideo. The bandsmen playing before the game enjoyed themselves so much the start of the match was delayed by about half an hour; Uruguay brought on new players at halftime (much frowned upon by the IRB's laws of the time) and spectators surged onto the field during the break, surrounding the players. Coaches then were not allowed to talk to their players at halftime but that was no impediment to the Uruguay coach, as Jack Gleeson noted from the stand with wry amusement.

One of the Uruguay players, Antonio Echeverra, let fly with a kick to the head of the All Black prop, John Spiers, and this initiated a short, sharp brawl that involved most of the players, some of the spectators and a couple of armed soldiers. The All Black fullback, Richard Wilson, was trying to calm down proceedings when he was confronted by a soldier wielding a knife. The alarmed Wilson retreated to the safety of his position.

After things cooled down, Echeverra was sent off but no one seemed to mind quarter of an hour later when he happily rejoined play and saw the match out.

It was during the stay in Uruguay that the players did without their daily allowance. It seemed that Argentina would not pay it because it wasn't their country and Uruguay would not pay it because they could not afford it. So the players went without, Ron Don persuading them to accept it all in the good name of rugby relations.

The tour began as it would continue, not with the brief burst of mayhem on the field but with the knowledge that this was a tour the like of which no All Black had experienced before. Frustration with travel arrangements and other aspects of organisation, always exacerbated by the language barrier, led to a gradual resigned amusement, to the point that no one, not even the hosts, expected anything to happen at the time it was supposed to happen.

At one point on a much-delayed train trip, Andy Haden and a couple of henchmen drew up a lengthy petition, demanding all manner of compensation and reparation, and presented it solemnly to the Uruguay union official who was with the team throughout, Carlos Uranga. He accepted it with the amusement and good grace in which it was offered. Nothing changed, though. It was on this same train trip that the locomotive was making such heavy weather of towing the carriages on the dead-flat terrain that Ian

Stevens leapt off and ran alongside for a while.

The All Blacks could not long be isolated from the political tension in Argentina. Ron Don laid down the law, both verbally and in writing, when the players first checked into their Buenos Aires hotel, the Alvear Palace, a grand old dame of a building that was redolent of 1920s stylish living and could have been straight from the set of the film *Evita*, which came out the following year. If someone calls 'Alto', Don said, that means stop. And you stop!

The country's army commander, Brigade General Jorge Rafael Videla, had seized power from the president, Isabel Peron, in a military coup a few months before the All Blacks arrived. It was a marked period of instability in Argentina's chequered political history. The All Blacks didn't want to know the details, but there were stories of underground terrorist attacks from both the left and the right and, even more sinister still, the government was said to be quick on the trigger when it came to detaining anyone who looked even the slightest bit suspicious.

All Blacks at different times were unwittingly and certainly unwillingly caught up in it. Four of the players, Richard Wilson, Paul Sapsford, Mervyn Jaffray and John Spiers, were once sitting in a café in Buenos Aires minding their own business when a man in civilian clothes walked in and pointed a pistol at them. A couple in the café who spoke English told the players the man was a policeman and he wanted them to leave. Jaffray produced his passport but the policeman was unimpressed. He kept pointing his pistol with one hand and gesticulating with the other and the players got out. Fast.

On another occasion, several of the players went for a run in downtown Buenos Aires and unknowingly strayed into an area where there had been a bomb explosion the day before. Heavily armed soldiers trained their weapons on them and shouted in Spanish; the players had no idea what was said but they got the message and the pace of their run increased markedly.

Military rule had its uses, though. One of the All Blacks' midweek matches was in Cordoba, 700 kilometres from Buenos Aires, and rather than an interminable train trip, the Argentine union arranged for the air force to take the team. The flight there was in a Hercules transport aircraft with the players sitting troop-like on fold-down metal seats with their backs to the bare fuselage of the aircraft. Bizarrely, the Hercules bore an RNZAF roundel on its fuselage, apparently a souvenir of a trip to Scott Base.

That flight was adventurous. Another was a little more so. The air force this time provided two DC-3s, the old twin-engined passenger aircraft that used to be known as the workhorse of the skies. Two were provided because the All Black party could not fit into one. This was a challenge to the Argentine pilots. The challenge, much to the horror of Ron Don and to some of the less adventurous travellers, was to see how close the aircraft could fly to each other. Looking from one aircraft to another, it seemed at times as if the wingtips were nearly touching. There was probably a safe enough margin between the two, but it served to concentrate the minds of the passengers.

The flight in the Hercules was from an airbase where there had been an attempt on the life of the president, Videla, a fortnight before and this was reported to New Zealand. A couple of weeks later, when the team was in Rosario, someone from the Reuters office in Buenos Aires phoned the reporter and told him the presidential palace was not pleased about the reference to the assassination attempt and that it would be wise for the reporter to stick purely to rugby matters.

The Reuters man added, unhelpfully, that the government's 'snatch squads' were active in Rosario and that they habitually drove green Vauxhalls. Chastened, the reporter stayed close to the bulk of Andy Haden for the rest of the stay in Rosario.

As can happen in a foreign country and when adverse conditions are met, the team was a close-knit one and several players as well as Don mentioned when they were home that team spirit, an important if difficult to define quality, was what got them through. It didn't just get them through, it also contributed to an unbeaten tour, something few saw as a likely outcome. And it also contributed, through Gleeson, Mourie, Haden and Wilson, to the success of the All Blacks for the next few years.